CHIEF

THE STORY OF A PIT BULL

A NOVEL

Duyen Nguyen

D1625581

CHIEF

THE STORY OF A PIT BULL

A NOVEL

Duyen Nguyen

PUBLISHED BY

 Escrire

A FICTION IMPRINT FROM ADDUCENT

Adducent, Inc.

www.Adducent.co

Titles Distributed In

North America

United Kingdom

Western Europe

South America

Australia

CHIEF

THE STORY OF A PIT BULL

A NOVEL

By Duyen Nguyen

ISBN: 9781937592486 (paperback)

Library of Congress Catalog Number: 2015937282

Published by Adducent, Inc. under its *Escrire* fiction imprint
Jacksonville, Florida
www.Adducent.Co

Published in the United States of America

Dedication & Acknowledgments

To all who love animals; your advocacy and action to save and protect them benefits our planet and humankind.

With special thanks to Dennis Lowery for his passionate and loving contribution to this work.

Table of Contents

SOME DEFINITIONS (all not necessarily used in the story)

The Keep: the training a fighting dog undergoes leading up to a fight, lasting about six weeks.

Gameness: tenacity and a willingness to fight (critical qualities for a fighting dog.)

Prospect: a young, aggressive dog identified as a potentially good fighting dog.

Campaign: a fighting dog's career.

Scratch Lines: lines in a dogfighting ring behind which the animals start in a match.

The Show: a dogfight.

Convention: a large dogfighting event that usually includes gambling (on site and remote) sometimes with accompanying activities like music and food.

Bait Dog: dogs that would not or could not fight. They were used as training tools. Dogmen often let their more aggressive dogs kill them as part of their training.

Champion: a dog who has won three fights.

Grand Champion: an undefeated dog with five wins.

Dogmen: professional trainers and handlers.

He who is cruel to animals becomes hard also in his dealings with men. We can judge the heart of a man by his treatment of animals.

--Immanuel Kant

OPENING

I was born into a world of violence. I didn't have a choice; no living thing can control the circumstances of their birth. But throughout my life, I found myself in situations where I could make choices. Some involved life and death decisions. I always made the one that saved others, even if I had to sacrifice myself. Even if I risked everything to do what was right. This is something humans should understand. All dogs are capable of nobility and honor. We are capable of acting in the same way that humans hold in the highest regard.

Most importantly, we are capable of love.

I learned that from two who are no longer with me. A little girl who gave me my first name and I hope she is somewhere very, very happy and far from the sad and tragic place we met. And a wonderful female of my own kind. She explained to me that love and respect connects all living things and to lose it once you have it is the worst tragedy. Respect bridges differences... love heals and through it, we become not merely a human and not just an animal—we become a person.

Without that—without them—I would never have met the woman who gave me my second name, Chief. She saved me... and I think I saved her.

1

NOVEMBER, 2005
NEAR PATTERSON, CALIFORNIA

I HATED THE CHAINS MOST. It's not like there was room in my cage to move around and maybe get some leverage to break out. It didn't matter; even inside the cage and pens... I wore chains. From the time I was a pup, I'd felt their weight. Light at first, and then increasingly heavier; sometimes, they crushed not just my body but also my spirit.

As I grew, the Dogman started adding heavier chains hooked to my collar. So heavy that the edges of the collar cut into my neck, forming a calloused ring. I wore them everywhere; while running, swimming and training with the Dogman, even in the fighting ring at practice. At night, I slept with them draped across my back and around my neck. As my body grew stronger, so did my thoughts of what controlled me; chains, cages... the Dogman. Was this how my life would be until I was killed?

Our cages were very close—dogs snarling at each other almost every minute of every day. I tried not to be that way. We all lived in a vast noise created by anger and pain and hunger. We were always hungry. Some dogs so hungry they would tear into any creature just to eat. I couldn't do that. I'd been beaten more than usual, because I would not kill the live rabbits dropped in the pit or into my cage. Even though it meant they would take the chains off. I'd be free from them, even if for just a short while when meat was there for me to take. But I couldn't do it.

Our training included having to tug, pull and hang from things the Dogman directed us to. Do it or be beaten. At first, it was a rope from a tree limb; then a tire swinging from a chain. Later, when I had grown large enough, it was a bag with a tough leather cover packed full of sand. I had torn through one and tasted the fine grain; it was not like dirt at all. The Dogman got excited when I did—he seemed very interested in how strong I was. Despite that, he still did not allow me to drink and wash away the grit in my mouth;

thirsty dogs bled less. But he didn't beat me afterwards. I guess that was some type of reward in his way of thinking.

At about ten months old, he started training me to develop my gameness. He wanted to make sure I could kill when he required me to.

* * *

My cage was close enough to see what was going on. The dog had not been hurt badly, and being bigger than the one he'd been matched with, if he'd fought back, he likely would not have been injured at all in the test match.

Afterwards, I saw the Dogman with him. He was shackled with more chains than I'd seen on any dog, even me and I thought I had carried the most. He was also muzzle-strapped, in a way different from what was normally used. This time, his jaws were pried apart and held open. The Dogman bent over him, back towards me, but I saw that he was pulling the dog's teeth out with a pair of pliers. Dropping each at his feet, the teeth lay there like small white and red jagged rocks with bits of pink flesh hanging on them. Blood ran from the dog's mouth, and urine and crap pooled around his hind feet. The Dogman was turning him into a bait dog.

Not many days after that, I had my first test match. My opponent was already in the ring. He stood still, but I saw the shake and quiver of his body. He had already urinated and defecated; signs of both streaked his hind quarters and legs. His paws were bloody and inflamed; the claws and nails had been torn out. I don't know how he could even stand. When he raised his bowed head, I saw the swollen face and eyes. It was the dog I'd seen the Dogman brutalize. He was to be my test; he was my bait dog to kill.

I couldn't do it. I wouldn't do it. I backed away; no matter how hungry I was, I would not do what the Dogman wanted. I turned my head to find him; to see where he perched watching us. Sitting in a chair he had to climb a half a dozen or so rungs of a ladder to get to, he made me always think of the big birds that I had seen circle the woods when he took a dog there and came back alone. I saw the Dogman's face tighten as he stared at me. He hopped down and approached me. I lowered my head, eyes never leaving him, but I broadened my stance. I knew what was coming. He was going to try to make me attack the bait dog. He'd beat me until I gave in or gave up.

He hit me in the rump with the lash he always carried attached to his wrist. It was heavy, with some kind of load inside a leather casing. I had felt it before and seen him break other dog's legs with it and one dog's back. It cracked like a rotten stick stepped on by a human's heavy boot. He flailed at me again and it struck across the broad part of my back. I blinked, shook my head, but didn't move. Moving wouldn't help. He hit me again and I felt my left hind leg go numb. The next blow would be on the face or head to stun me. Then he would drag me off into the woods to kill me, or chain me and yank out my teeth and claws to face the same fate of the broken dog still shaking five feet away.

The next blow didn't land. A crazed dog, probably near starving to death, had broken free from a pen nearby and jumped into the ring to tear at the bait dog. I looked at it standing there defenseless and hopeless. I was expected to attack this poor shaking victim... a dog just like me. Instead, I fought for him.

I didn't know at the time that by saving him, I actually saved myself.

* * *

After that, I routinely ended up on what the Dogman called 'the Keep.' I'd heard him say that several times to the young man that did errands for him and handled some of the dogs. He would run me for an hour or more each day with a 40-pound chain attached to my collar. Over time, he used an even heavier chain. Then he'd make me swim for another hour in an above-ground pool that always had green scum floating on top. I couldn't keep it out of my eyes, nose and mouth. I hardly had time to sneeze and cough it out before the Dogman would move me onto another task. Another exercise or drill. Sometimes he would give me pills and other times would stick me with needles. Day in and day out it never changed.

2

NOVEMBER 2, 2005
NEAR RAMADI, IRAQ

"SMALL ARMS FIRE. THIS COULD GET ROUGH, CHIEF..."
Hannah Arshakunian called to her gunner and
copilot, Chief Warrant Officer Michael Smathers who
sat lower and in front of her in the nose. As she
pitched their AH-64 Apache out of low bird position
and away from the incoming rounds, the cockpit
sidewall Plexiglas and floor shredded. They went into
a slow spin. "I can't hold it... Can't..."

The ground was coming up fast. It was if they
were frozen, unmoving, and it was racing towards
them. Another blast from below shook the helicopter
and a ball of flame flared and rolled across the nose of
the Apache. Hannah stomped for the control pedals,
trying to get it aligned to hit flat bottom down where

9

the airframe was strongest. Nothing. The trim pedals weren't working. She looked to see if something was jamming them.

"Shit... Mike." When she looked down, she saw a gaping hole beneath her rimmed with shredded metal. Then she realized her leg was gone. Her flight suit on that side was slick with a stream of splattered blood still slinging from the ragged fabric. "My leg... my leg. It must've dropped through that big freaking hole." She called to Mike. "Chief..."

"Hannah..." his voice came back tight with pain but she had no idea how badly he had been wounded.

With each gyration of the helicopter, she felt something flap near her nose and swiped the back of her hand across it. It came away with even more blood. The skin, one side of her face, had been peeled back. It flapped; the end of a bloody scarf, all the way down her neck when she bent her head. She wondered why it only stung. But she'd seen many men and women wounded. She knew all the pain, the bad shit, would come later.

They hit the ground at an angle as she reached to shut off the four blades. The trail of another incoming RPG made her jerk back in her harness as she squirmed to try to release it. Its impact dislodged the cockpit shell in front of her and she saw the flames wash over Mike. His seat and body came free in the blast and shifted back, pinning her down. But it also shielded her from the fire. She smelled him burning and thanked god he was unconscious. Blood covered her face and she fought to free her right arm from underneath her body. She tried to bring the left arm up to wipe her eyes. The scream was louder than the sound of the dying and burning metal around her. She realized it was hers just before everything went dark.

* * *

The medic had gotten there shortly after the impact. He had known she wouldn't survive a medevac and got her to a Forward Surgical Team. She had lost her left leg above the knee; her left arm had been sliced open from shoulder to elbow and it looked like the shredded forearm was broken. The left side of her face, from hairline down her neck to the shoulder and around onto her back was a bloodied mangle of flesh.

She was in what combat medics call the golden hour when the worst wounds had to be treated or the person wouldn't survive. She had lost more than half the blood in her body. He pumped plasma, antibiotics and steroids into her. The FST got her stabilized for transfer to the CASH in Baghdad. Hers was one of many helos that came in around the clock at Iraq's busiest hospital for United States personnel.

* * *

NOVEMBER 25, 2005
10TH COMBAT SUPPORT HOSPITAL (CASH), BAGHDAD

The tick tick tick of equipment seemed loud in a room that wasn't completely dark. There was a glow from different monitors... breathing, heart rate, blood pressure in an array of red and green. On one, she saw a blinking crawl of yellow across the bottom of the display. She didn't know what in the hell that was.

Her eyes felt sticky, like they'd been closed for a long time. She tried to rub them but the left was covered with a thick bandage that ran around her head, down her neck and onto her chest. She managed to clear the right eye and could see better now. Raising her head, in the dimness, she looked down the length of her body. She tried to sit up and grunted; the damn IV and other things stuck in and on her pulled and tugged as she moved.

Her left shoulder and arm were heavily bandaged from armpit to elbow and below that was a cast that covered the forearm to her wrist. It hurt like hell to move, so she left it at her side and reached over and flipped the sheet off with her right arm. She felt where it should be. Yep. Everything from mid-thigh down was gone. "They've taken my left fucking leg." She cried.

She ripped the leads off her chest and fingertips— the IV from her right forearm came out dangling by its tape. A jagged flash of pain lanced along the side of her face and neck as she bent forward and tried to sit up. Her vision started to gray out as she gripped the stump of her leg. She realized she shouldn't have; it wasn't as if she could pull on it and her leg would suddenly extrude like Play-Doh. Or that it would grow back if she only willed it to hard enough. It hurt. Bad. Her face and neck stung. She raised a hand and pulled way the tape and gauze.

Her fingers traced the stitches from the left side of her neck up under the chin to curve across her cheek. They ran past the edge of the eye into her short cropped, dark-auburn, hair. There at her left temple was a depression; it felt a little spongy as if a piece of bone was gone. Christ! She felt the scooped divots of flesh peppered around her cheek. She started to swing her leg off the bed and almost made it. She was close to passing out. That's when the nurses got to her. She didn't fight. Didn't have any left in her, but they held her arms down and got the IV back in. One added something from a hypodermic to it and soon everything went black.

3

MARCH, 2006

NEAR PATTERSON, CALIFORNIA

THE DIGITAL SCALE WAS THE NEWEST PIECE OF
EQUIPMENT THE DOGMAN OWNED. They had to be
precise, so he'd replaced the old ones he'd had for
years. He had built a reputation among his peers—the
players and kingpins of an illegal dogfighting network
that stretched from Maine to Florida, across the
United States to California and up to Washington
State—that he was someone they could rely on; a man
to watch on the west coast.

He was close to hosting his first Convention;
the biggest of events for a dogman. Everything leading
up to it had to be top notch. Dogmen were like
members of a secret society; their Shows were
invitation-only. Those spectators invited were not

informed of the Show's location until an hour or so before it was to begin—sometimes less. He had the location and the infrastructure. He'd invested in computers and had a system set to send out email invitations to his private mailing list. They usually drove to the shows in cars or trucks with the license plates removed to avoid being identified and he had a special area cleared and marked for them.

On top of that, he had someone that would do a heat run; checking the way to his Shows, doubling back on the route to see if any cops were following in an unmarked vehicle. If there was one, or anything looked wrong or suspicious, they could cancel instantly and a text message would go out warning the participants to not come. He was setting things up right and the big boys, even some from Vegas, were watching him.

He turned to look out over his operations, viewing in his mind more than with his eyes, all the things he had bought and built... the rows of cages and training pits. And the buffer of private land that ensured that most of his site was shielded from prying eyes.

This match was part of that process. He looked down at the dog under his hands; it might be his ticket to an even bigger piece of the pie. A champion—then grand champion—it could happen. As a pup, the Dogman had thought of this dog as The Mask because of its markings; a black cowl covering cheeks, eyes and ears. But his daughter had taken to calling it Hero. That name stuck in his head, though he never used it. Dogs were objects or products. And he had doubts about this dog.

If this dog, Hero, lived he could be positioned as a breeder. He had some pieces of that puppy mill already in place; a separate area for breeding stands and a source of clean, strong, females. Things just needed to go as planned and he'd make a fortune. He looked down at the dog again and got back to the work at hand.

The dogs weighed in, each suspended from the scale with a thin cord running under front legs and chest. "Fifty-two pounds." The Dogman called out Hero's weight and the other dog's handler confirmed. They switched places as the handler brought his dog, Razorblade, onto the scale. An all-white pit bull with a jagged pink lightning bolt of a scar that ran across his head past the ears onto the neck. Others crisscrossed his thick chest and a patchwork of them decorated his left hindquarter. Razorblade was a force locally. He had what they called a hard mouth; he was a vicious biter.

"Fifty-eight pounds." The Dogman confirmed—Hero's opponent was larger. Those scars, and that he still fought despite having received them, showed he would be hard to beat. He looked at Hero; younger and without competitive fight scars from the Show. But then, at 15-months-old, this was his first real fight.

The Dogman and the other handler exchanged dogs and took them to the wash basin. 'Cajun Rules' called for them, the owners or their handlers, to wash each other's dogs, using the same mix of water, baking soda, warm milk, and vinegar to make sure their coats were not treated with any foreign substance that would inhibit biting. Each then dried the other's dog with towels and a blanket that the other provided.

They took the dogs to the fighting pit. This was one of his smallest; only eight feet square but it had the higher three feet walls. The Dogman had intentionally picked this for Hero's first genuine fight. This pit would keep them in close; force them to be on each other without much room to avoid the other dog. He needed to see if Hero... if it had the true stuff of a potential champion. During a test, though starved, it had not gone after the bait dog. That usually meant he would have to put it down, sooner rather than later, or use it as bait with one of the larger, aggressive, dogs he was training. He had been about to cage it again, probably to take it to the woods later, when Jawbreaker, an intense, crazed dog that even he disliked being around, jumped the bait dog in the pit test match with Hero.

Jawbreaker was fearless and easily twelve pounds heavier. The Dogman knew better than to get between him and another dog—especially a bait dog. Jawbreaker had a reputation as a leg dog, a bone breaker. He'd come in low, rip out a chunk off one leg to slow the dog down and immediately tear into the other leg, trying to break it quickly and get the dog on the ground for the kill. He had expected Hero to be quickly shredded, too. There wasn't much chance of him surviving, the Dogman thought.

But that didn't happen. Hero had backed up to get his butt against the wall behind him, never turning his head or trying to twist away. He then charged Jawbreaker, knocking him off the bait dog and rolling him several feet away. Jawbreaker came up fast, his lower teeth extended and snapping out, just like that alien in the movies. Hero had gotten low underneath his jaws, turned his own up, and clamped onto Jawbreaker's neck. Surging up, he pivoted and slammed Jawbreaker into the ground, then whipped him into a cage wall pinning him where he struggled, but couldn't break free. Hero had taken a slash across his face in that initial attack. He stood there bleeding heavily from it; his blood pouring on the dog beneath him.

The Dogman remembered thinking as he took Jawbreaker to the woods that day, maybe this dog... Hero... might have something to him. He would give him more time.

And he had. This match would be a true test. Razorblade was already at his scratch line as he brought Hero forward to his. He would soon know whether he had a prospect. Maybe one that could even take down The Devil; Lee Boucher's prize dog—the sonofabitch.

"Face your dogs," said the referee. Razorblade's head slunk low on his shoulders, and his paws strained, pulling against his handler. The referee shouted, "Release your dogs!"

Razorblade flew across the ring; a terrifying flash of teeth and bunched, powerful muscle slammed into Hero, fangs slicing at his face. The impact shook them both as Razorblade bit in and ripped up. Blood spurting from his mouth and chest, Hero got to his feet. More blood and urine drenched the ground. His right front leg was already wounded and with the gash up his chest and neck to his bottom lip, he had trouble standing. He steadied and straightened as Razorblade came at him again.

* * *

That first fight had lasted nearly two hours. The Dogman looked at his watch as he stitched up Hero, who stood there legs locked and in a muzzle that clamped his jaws shut. The worst wound ran down the right side of his face and along the side of his neck, then across his chest to between his front legs. The Dogman had just finished stitching the equally ugly tear that ran across his back, curving off to his right side to end just above his stomach. He shook his head, not knowing how the dog had survived.

Razorblade had done a job on Hero but he'd received several new scars of his own. A weakened, nearly dead on his feet, Hero had pinned him against the pit wall, subduing, but not killing him. Razorblade's handler had a disgusted look as they separated the two when the ref called the win in favor of Hero.

The Dogman shook his own head at a dog that could win but would not kill. He scratched his nose, leaving a smear of Hero's blood on it. He looked up and saw his daughter, Amy, watching them. She'd climbed up his chair and looked down on them while he worked. Her face was white as he bent to run water over Hero to check the stitches and for any other damage. He would fight him again in a month or so.

* * *

MAY, 2006

The second fight was going to run even longer than Hero's first. It was two hours in and the Dogman had already unfanged Hero twice—pulling the lip away to see where it was wedged and then with a quick slice of his knife cutting it away, leaving chunks of flesh stuck in his teeth. But the lip was now free.

Hero's face was a scarlet mask now; neck and chest covered in blood. It poured from his mouth and his bared teeth had a wet ruby gleam. A large flap of flesh, torn from just two inches above his right eye, hung down. Red and ragged, it added to the stream blinding him and making him slower to reach to an opponent that was already much faster. Rocket had rolled him over to strike at his stomach. The slash was shallow in the front, between his forelegs, and grew deeper as it got to his back legs near his privates. Blood poured on the ground from it.

Over the past month of preparing him, the Dogman had forbidden Amy to watch Hero fight. He was glad he had made that decision. The dog she was so interested in wouldn't survive this one. Rocket was too fast and was relatively undamaged. Hero was bleeding out. Rocket had him against the wall when

Hero's head dropped, twisting his neck free to bring his teeth up under Rocket's head at the bend of the jaw were it joined the neck. With a powerful lift and push, Hero slung him up and over; showering the Dogman with his blood. Hero slammed Rocket into the ground, keeping his jawlock on him, and tractor plowed him across the pit to the far wall. Smashing him into immobility at the feet of his handler, Hero held Rocket there, barely able to stand, until the ref called the win.

The Dogman quickly swung his legs over the wall and went to Hero. He had to stop the bleeding. If he could save him, this dog might stand a chance against The Devil... and if Hero could beat The Devil then the Dogman's fortune was made. He would be famous. He'd get those Vegas boys lined up and money would pour in. "Jumping Jesus, it would be Christmas every day." He muttered to himself. If his hands hadn't been covered in dog blood he'd have clapped them and danced a jig.

4

MAY, 2006
WALTER REED NATIONAL MILITARY MEDICAL CENTER
BETHESDA, MARYLAND

HANNAH KNEW WHY THE FIELD SURGICAL TEAM HAD JUST
ROUGH STITCHED HER UP. Speed and getting the
bleeding stopped were more important than
aesthetics. And now she knew that wounds, especially
facial, had to heal fully before they were remodeled by
a plastic surgeon. So she had been sutured together.
Then she'd had a seizure or stroke at Ramstein in
German brought on by cerebral edema, brain
swelling, and had been in a coma for five months.
Transferred here, to Walter Reed, she'd finally come
out of the coma to face being cut open again now that

they were sure the brain swelling was not going to recur. This time she hoped for a better result.

She was stretched out on an operating table trying not to be blinded by the bright light almost directly over her face. "What's that?" she asked. The doctor had said something to her.

"These are going to sting... and like I told you before this is going to take a while and it will be very uncomfortable for you." The surgeon bent over her with a hypodermic in hand. "Are you sure you don't want me to use general anesthesia?"

Hannah had had enough of being unconscious. "No, just get started, doc... the sooner it's done the better."

It did sting. Each injection had a sharp bite, as he pushed the needle in and out, relocating and repeating the process following the path of the red seam that formed the tree trunk of the scar. It was thicker on her face and thinner with branches running from it as it ran all the way down her neck to end with a gouged out area of missing flesh just above the clavicle. The injections were supposed to deaden the area, but she knew they wouldn't completely numb. The memory of pain would get in the way and she would feel the scalpel as it made the new cuts; some of the incisions directly into the new not long healed scars.

She had heard about it from other veterans in rehab that had gone through similar operations. The surgeon would pull and tuck, smoothing the flesh into something more pleasing than its current ragged, puckered, appearance and then would sew it in place.

She closed her eyes and tried not to think about the next step; a second surgery on her left leg stump to remove neuromas, a cluster of nerves that kept her in pain. That had to heal and then they would fit her with a prosthetic leg. She would go through the first phase of rehabilitation, getting used to the prosthetic to become ambulatory. Then they would transfer to the Veterans Administration hospital closest to her home town or place of permanent residence. She knew she was headed to San Francisco since it was only an hour or two from her home town. Great. I'm going home. The thought did not make her happy.

"Shit..." she muttered at the sharp stab of pain.

"Sorry." the surgeon said quietly, hands not stopping or pausing. But he didn't sound like he meant it.

5

AUGUST, 2006
NEAR PATTERSON, CALIFORNIA

HER STEPFATHER DIDN'T LIKE IT. Not even when he was down there with them. Her friends had them as pets; they told funny stories about things they had done and always talked about playing with them. She loved to hear about that. She wasn't supposed to be online, but she had seen some of their pictures on that website her mother liked, Facebook. She couldn't look at them long though; her mom might catch her and she would be in trouble. But the pictures were so cute!

She wished she had one, a puppy to hold when she wanted, to play with and maybe sleep in her room. She had tried talking to her stepdad about it. "Please, all my friends have pets."

"No, Amy." He shook his head, already angry. "We can't have other animals messing around the place and leaving scent. And the dogs, they're for business and don't you tell anyone about them." He stood and loomed over her. "You best listen to what I say and mind me."

He was scary when he was like that and her mom always got a worried look. "It's okay, Lloyd..." She looked at me and I knew she wanted me to be quiet; to shut my mouth about pets or dogs, anything that might get him riled. "She won't say anything."

But she wanted to have a dog of her own so badly. One just like...

* * *

"Hero," she called. It was late. The moon was behind the clouds, and it was dark down by the pens. She couldn't see far; her flashlight had a piece of light blue plastic taped over the end to cut the glare. She couldn't risk her mom, or worse, her stepdad getting up for a drink or late snack, looking out the kitchen window, and seeing a light where it shouldn't be.

She knew he was expecting her. It had been going on for a while now, since he was a pup in his own cage. "Hero," she whispered louder. She heard him first and then saw him in the dim light. The white of his muzzle; cheeks and eyes surrounded by dark fur that mixed with the shadows... the mask of his face that prompted her name for him. Just like the heroes in stories and cartoons she adored.

"Good boy..." She knelt next to his cage. Her hand was barely small enough to reach in and stroke his head. She took out a plastic baggy with bacon she'd saved from breakfast and a couple of slices of cheese from dinner. She knew he was always hungry. A word she had heard on television came to her, as she watched him gobble down the scraps and nuzzled her hand looking for more. Something she saw on one of the cable channels. Her mother said it was a documentary; and turned it off when she saw her watching it.

The man in it had been talking about something called the Holocaust and concentration camps. She didn't understand what that meant, but the people it showed, behind an ugly wire fence, had looked starved and beat up. The man talking about them said that word she hadn't heard before. It must mean how the people looked to him. It was a scary sounding word and the man had sounded so sad as he talked. When he said it, she knew it must be awful to be that way. To be that word.

"Gaunt." She whispered to herself as she looked at him under the dim light. She leaned close, against the wire, and he turned to press the side of his body against the cage. She felt ribs but also the bunched powerful muscles of his neck shoulders and legs—and the scars; ridges and seams, that ran across his body.

He turned his head, backing away a bit to lie down, head near her hand. He licked her fingers.

"I know boy... I love you, too." She always cried, but she needed to leave him soon. She could never stay more than a few minutes. And though it always hurt to go, she would be back. She lay down to face him; nose to nose, as she had always done since he was a pup. Her face against the bars he licked her nose and the tears from her cheeks. She rose from the ground, new tears forming. "I'll see you tomorrow night." She wiped her cheeks with the palm of her hand and sleeve of her shirt. "I miss you, always..." She backed away into the night before turning towards the house.

* * *

I thought about her as I lay in the mud and muck of my cage. When she first came to me, it was before my real training started. I knew who she was. She was family to the Dogman. How could that be? How she could be nice with her father being such a very mean man? I didn't understand. I didn't know why the little girl came to visit me. No one ever had; not even once before her. No one had ever talked to me as she did. Tenderly and with kindness.

She would reach through the cage and touch me. No one ever had done it as she did; softly. I thought she was the only reason I didn't lie down and let what was surely going to happen to me happen sooner. Why hold on? Did I because of her? Because of those few moments in the dark with a human that did not want to hurt me. Someone that did not want me to hurt other dogs. She was the only human I knew that cared for me.

I thought that's why I wanted to live.

* * *

A light rain was falling but the girl didn't seem to mind. The poncho with its hood kept off the water and it helped hide the light in her lap. She didn't shine it on me. It was tilted up, against her chest, to show her face.

"Here boy." She slid the biscuit between the bars. I carefully took it from her hand, gulped it down, and hoped for more. She reached into the inside pocket of the poncho and pulled another out. "Last one; it's all I could get tonight."

With one chew, I swallowed it too, my stomach rumbling. We were never fed well, but even less before fights; just enough so we were not weakened but not enough to satisfy. Constant hunger kept us on aggressive edge was the Dogman's belief. And he usually gave us very little water; I felt how going without it made my skin tighter. Maybe that made it harder for the other dog to bite and get a good grip.

She heard my stomach growl again, louder this time. "I'm sorry I don't have more for you..."

I looked at her face. The light slanting up caught the wetness on her cheeks not caused by rain.

"He's been really bad lately; I can't do or say anything without him getting on to me. He screamed at mother about wasting food the other night. So she's watching things too."

I watched as she wiped her face with a paper towel from her pocket. It came apart in her hands. I was tired and soaked by the rain, but moved closer to put my head against the bars. She stroked the mud matted hair of my head and neck. The summer nights were warm and muggy; the mud was still sticky and smeared her fingers and hands. She rubbed her nose, leaving a smudge of it just below her eyes.

"Mom says he's that way because of the Convention; that's when he has a lot of people here for the fights." I knew she was talking about the Dogman by her tone. She waved a hand towards where the new fighting pit had been prepared. "She says he talks like he'll make a bunch of money from it." She looked down into the beam of light then up at me. "Hero, this morning I heard him tell mom that he's counting on you to win... he has a lot of money bet on you because the odds are so good. And if you do, you'll be a champion with three wins. That means even more money for him next time you fight."

She stopped talking and looked down again. I could hear the tempo of the drops of rain landing on her poncho increase and felt more of them on my head and back but still didn't move. There wasn't much shelter for me in my cage anyway.

"But if you keep fighting you could die, and if you don't, he'll..."

I heard her crying inside the hood and saw her shoulders shake.

"He'll kill you." She shifted the light to her watch and looked up. I knew what that meant. She needed to go; it was past time. "It's tomorrow, the big fight..." She knelt in the mud and slid her slender arms through the bars to hug my neck tight; pulling me closer to her against the bars. "Please don't die!"

* * *

AUGUST, 2006

WALTER REED HOSPITAL
BETHESDA, MARYLAND

"It's time." The rehabilitation therapist she'd met the day before stuck his head in her room.

"I'll be with you in a minute, Ted." Hannah told him and turned to her parents. It was time for the conversation she had been avoiding. They had both risen from their chairs.

"We'll see you later then... okay, Hannah?" Her dad sounded certain and her mom looked hopeful. She knew what she was about to say would hurt them both, but she had to tell them.

She took a deep breath. "I'd rather not... I think you should head home." There was a moment of dead silence as they looked at her. Her mother's eyes were welling with soon to be shed tears. The hurt was in her father's eyes, too.

"You don't have to go through this alone." Her father's voice said it all. He'd been the one to suggest, and then badger her to join the Air National Guard. He had served in the Army and it had been what turned his life around and gave it focus. He thought it would do the same for her and now he would never forgive himself for what had happened.

She knew this would come across as her way of punishing him; by pushing them away. The truth was after only a few days back in the United States, here with them at the hospital, she felt more wounded and ugly. On her own she would be anonymous; just another wounded and disfigured veteran among hundreds. She waved a hand around the room, clearly also meaning beyond the walls. "I'm not alone; I have lots of company here..." She couldn't help the bitterness in her voice but tried to cover it. "I'll get through this stage and they said I'll then transfer to the VA hospital near home. Probably in about 90 days. So that puts me in Santa Cruz just before Thanksgiving. Carol will meet me there. I'll do my final rehab, they'll discharge me and then maybe you can come for the holiday." Her tone didn't leave it open for discussion or debate.

Her father started to say something, stopped and turned without speaking. He reached for his wife's arm and they left. Her mother paused at the door making her husband turn with her. "Never forget that we love you, Hannah."

* * *

"I have to give you the prep talk and overview, so sorry for the speech and jargon." Ted warned her. "Rehabilitation teaches ambulation skills—that means getting around on your prosthetic. It includes exercises to improve general conditioning and balance, to stretch the hip and knee, to strengthen all extremities, and to help you tolerate the prosthesis. Because ambulation requires a 10 to 40% increase in energy expenditure after below-the-knee amputation and a 60 to 100% increase after above-the-knee amputation, endurance exercises may be needed."

He stopped and nodded at her. "You're an above-the-knee so you already had extra work to do. With the coma, all that time flat on your back, you need even more strength work. Now that you're medically stable, rehabilitation will start to help prevent secondary disabilities. That's where you're at now so we're going to begin standing and doing balancing exercises with parallel bars when we're done with this overview." He pointed at the set of bars and mats behind him.

"We also have to work on flexibility. Flexion contracture of the hip or knee may develop rapidly, making fitting and using the prosthesis difficult;

contractures can be prevented with extension braces made by occupational therapists. So expect that. We also have to teach you how to care for the stump and how to recognize the earliest signs of skin breakdown. Then we have to condition your stump. Stump conditioning promotes the natural process of shrinking that must occur before a prosthesis can be used.

"After only a few days of conditioning, the stump may have shrunk greatly. An elastic shrinker or elastic bandages worn 24 hours a day can help taper the stump and prevent edema. The shrinker is easy to apply, but bandages may be preferred because they better control the amount and location of pressure. But, application of elastic bandages requires skill, and bandages must be reapplied whenever they become loose. Pay attention to this so we can work with you and your stump to get you fitted as soon as possible. Early ambulation with a temporary prosthesis helps start exercises on the parallel bars and progress to walking with crutches or canes until a permanent prosthesis is made. For above-the-knee amputees, several knee-locking options are available according to the patient's skills and activity level. Some newer technologies include microprocessor-controlled knee and ankle joints that enable patients to adjust movement as needed. We'll have to see what works best for you. Any questions?"

"What about taking care of this..." Hannah pointed at her stump. "After I leave the hospital."

"Well you're two or three months away from that barring any problems. But at bedtime, the stump should be inspected thoroughly, with a mirror so you can check the underside, too, and washed with mild soap and warm water. Then you dry it thoroughly and dust it with talcum powder. We'll go through all of that with you step by step." He moved over to a table with several different legs. "Let's get your temp on and then up on the bars you go." He paused and looked at her. "You ready for this?"

She nodded her head yes, but inside... her mind said, no.

6

LATE SEPTEMBER, 2006
NEAR PATTERSON, CALIFORNIA

MY CAGE WAS CLOSEST TO THE NEW RING AND I SAW THEM UNLOAD THE DEVIL. The two humans were large men and wore protection on their hands and arms; the kind handlers wore in the pit when working with dogs. They slid the huge cage out of the rear of a white, box-shaped, machine that had backed in a few minutes ago. As it came into the sunlight, I saw the dark shape that filled it. The dog inside was the biggest I'd ever seen. Its growl, a dark cloud's thunder, carried the distance to me and I could feel the menace. The two men did not look happy to be so close, and hurried to set the cage down as quickly as they could and move away.

The Dogman was standing nearby, and stepped towards the cage once they had it on the ground. He looked at the beast inside and then up in my direction. I knew what that look meant.

Another man got out of the front of the white machine. He had something held to his ear and talked into it. After a moment, he put it in his pocket and walked over to the Dogman. They nodded at each other but I didn't see them grip hands as I had seen him do with other humans when he met or greeted them. The Devil next to them screamed and the Dogman moved away. The other man put his hand on the cage and smiled at the Dogman.

* * *

THE FIGHT

With the first thrust of contact, Devil's teeth had torn a six inch gash in my left shoulder. I had felt his teeth clink on the bones in the joint as they ripped through the muscle. I was used to pain, but all of it piled on over the last year and a half had made me want to lie down and quit; too tired to keep going. But if I quit, Devil would kill me now or if the Dogman stopped the fight, he would kill me later. I had seen it done many times—an old dog or one just not a fighter—used as a bait dog or taken deeper into the woods. That was always followed by a single sharp crack; a sound that echoed but would be ignored in the woods. Even if a trespasser chanced to be nearby. The Dogman always came back alone.

This wasn't the same as my other two fights. I had seen the look in the Dogman's eye. No matter what, if I didn't fight and win, I was going to die.

Despite that, I did not want to fight. At the start signal, I had turned away from Devil. At that turn from my opponent, the referee stopped the fight and the Dogman and Devil's handler took us back behind our scratch lines. We would re-start. The Dogman's face was red and hot-eyed. He glared at me. I knew this would not end; the pain would never end until I was dead.

I shook my head, feeling the deep puncture in my gashed shoulder. Devil was bleeding from what was left of his right ear and a gash in his neck. In that first lunge, when he ripped my shoulder open, it hurt far more than any wound before, and in reflex, I had gotten a good bite in, tearing a chunk of flesh from him. But Devil was bigger, stronger, and far crueler than I would ever be—and he loved to fight. That wound didn't even slow him down. I saw him quiver as his handler restrained him, with a rage as dark as his fur. His eyes had gone completely black; like he had become evil incarnate, no longer an animal. The next lunge from him would be to tear open my throat. The win would make him a Grand Champion; the most prized and feared of all the local fighters.

Blood and sweat ran into my eyes as I shook my head trying to clear it. I know the little girl was watching. I couldn't see her, but her scent was in the air. I knew she was out there somewhere. I wanted to look around; to scan the crowd of human faces, men mostly but a few women too, with open mouths and loud voices. I wanted to see the girl before I died but knew that would not happen. "I'm sorry," I bayed. I bared my teeth at the Devil, ready for his charge. The man in the pit raised his hand about to signal the re-start.

An earsplitting sound rolled over us. A roar of a bullhorn and screech of a human voice shouting commands that stopped everyone and everything. I raised my head and looked away from the pit. I saw Devil do the same; pivoting to find the source of the sound and loud voice. The humans were running everywhere. The Dogman kicked the pit gate open and ran for the woods, following the men and women fleeing the area.

The men approaching the pit wore dark clothes that looked the same. Still shouting, they surrounded the area and started putting what looked like small chains on the hands of the people involved in the fight. In the chaos and confusion, I broke for the forest. The tree line and heavy brush were not that far. I topped the pit wall and saw the Devil at my side. Snarling and growling, he evaded a man to our right trying to drop a wire loop on him. Not wanting to be near that demon dog, I veered off at an angle. I had just cleared the pen area when I saw her. The girl was kneeling behind my pen, out of sight of anyone coming that way.

I ran to her.

"No Hero, no! Get away from me!"

I skidded to a stop just short of her. There had always been bars or wire mesh between us. I inched closer to her. Looking down at me, her tears came harder, the sobs louder. Finally, she knelt to hug me tight.

"You have to go, run, Hero!" She pushed me away towards the woods, my blood smearing on her hands.

Licking her hand and trying to rub my head on her leg, I didn't understand and held my ground. She pushed me harder and I looked at her. A shout made me turn and look back the way I had come—from the fighting pit. A man with a gun in his hand was running towards us. I realized what the girl had been scared about.

"Go!" The girl pushed me again, hard.

I knew she was right. With a last nuzzle of my nose against her leg, I bolted into the brush. Once out of sight, I slowed so as not to make any noise. Behind me I heard the banshee howl of a crazed dog and a human's scream. The girl! I turned and raced back.

As I broke through the thick grass and bush, I saw the girl backed against the wall of the building the Dogman used for food storage. In front of her, the man with the gun was down on his back on the ground. The Devil astride his chest had torn gaping wounds in his arms, shoulders, and throat. Growling bloody foam, the Devil rose from the twitching body of the man and approached the girl. She screamed again.

I charged in, launching myself at the beast. I lowered my head and got my jaws around his throat as we slammed into the wall. Slinging the Devil around, twisting the larger dog, I dug in to drag him farther away from the girl.

"No!" the girl screamed.

The man did not realize I was trying to protect the girl. I saw him rise on one elbow and aim his gun at us. He fired and blew a hole in the Devil's head; the back of his skull became a gaping cavity. The next shot went through my neck and plowed a deep rip from shoulder to tail.

The girl screamed at me again, "Run Hero!"

I looked at her, then at the man who was trying to aim the gun again and ran for the woods.

7

END SEPTEMBER, 2006

FRANK RAINES PARK
NEAR PATTERSON, CALIFORNIA

I HAD SLEPT OUTSIDE MY ENTIRE LIFE BUT NEVER IN THE OPEN AND UN-CAGED. Since the fight, it'd been light, dark, and light again. As I traveled, I had watched the bright circle in the sky climb and then go down. It was going down again and the woods were growing dark.

I had found water, a little stream that I now followed; it was leading me to where I didn't know. It was just away. Away from the Dogman; away from the fighting and the pain. Though I still hurt, I hoped at some point the pain would stop. I had lain in the cool water of the stream. I let it wash the tear in my shoulder, the longer, deeper, rip across and shoulder along my back to my rump and the other lesser cuts. I'd just sit there for a little while and then move on.

I awoke with a jerk. I had fallen asleep in the sun. I'd left the cries and calls from humans and other dogs behind me, but I knew I needed to keep moving. I needed to find... What? I wasn't sure. I just didn't know.

In the last dark time, night the light-haired little girl had called it, I looked for her and bayed. Calling and calling for her, no one answered. I was alone even more than when I was in my cage. I felt a far deeper ache than any bite that had left me scarred. Where was she? Where was I?

* * *

EARLY OCTOBER, 2006

WEST OF THE BLUE OAK RANCH RESERVE
NEAR SAN JOSE, CALIFORNIA

Even the cooling of sundown didn't help; I still felt hot and couldn't stop panting. My shoulder was swollen and throbbing but at least the bleeding had slowed. I had torn open the rip from the man's bullet. I'd been turning when it hit me, enough I guess to affect its path through fur and flesh. By twisting my head, I could see part of it where the edges had crusted with dried blood.

I pushed through the heavy brush and felt it snag and pull the wound. Stiff, sharp branches scored my sides with new scratches; the stouter limbs stabbed and gouged me. Soon I was bleeding heavily again.

I knew that the big light in the sky, the little girl had called it the sun, came up from the ground behind me. Back that way was where the Dogman lived. I had followed the sun as it rose in the sky to fall ahead of me; always moving never stopping for long unless I passed out. That was the direction I'd followed for days, stumbling towards I didn't know what. I kept going that way even though the small stream had veered off. I hadn't had a drink in a long time. My nose felt hot and my lips were dried and cracked. Flies and gnats, low to the ground and thick in the brush, clustered around my eyes. I kept blinking and stopping to rub them with a paw. It helped only for a second and then they were back.

I had fallen—gotten up—fallen to get up again more times than I could remember. I was so tired. Why did getting up matter. No one cared. I remembered something the little girl had said to me; she'd asked me not to die. Some part inside, I didn't know if it was hope or stubbornness, wouldn't let me lay there. So I got up each time. Until finally I couldn't.

* * *

Something nosed me on my back and brought me awake. I jerked up, managed to get on my legs and staggered. I had bled again. The dried blood and dirt clotted my side. As I got my footing and backed away, I felt stiff hairs around the wound pull as I moved.

It was a large dog with a once handsome coat now matted, full of burrs and bits of bark and grass. It bared its teeth and their length told me it was much older than I was. I sniffed. Female? As I backed further away, she lowered her lips covering her teeth. "I won't hurt you." She sank to the ground and put her head between her paws. Her eyes never left mine.

"Who are you... what are you doing here?" I scanned the woods but only heard birds in the trees above us; nothing else moved that I could tell. She raised her head to look at me.

"I'm Ellie." I cocked my head and she knew I didn't understand her. "That's my human name. My owners gave it to me when they brought me home."

She sounded pleased at having a human name and owners. I couldn't quite comprehend that. I shook my head as a wave of weakness came over me. I heard the other dog, Ellie, move and snapped my eyes up. I saw she was moving off in the direction I'd been heading before I had to stop. My eyes blurred again and I sank to the ground. The day went black around me.

* * *

Something woke me. Water was dripping on my mouth. I opened it, taking in a small amount. Then I sniffed... I smelled food. I opened my eyes and not a foot in front of my nose was the dog I'd seen before passing out. Ellie. Her muzzle was wet and between her paws, spread flat and held open by them, was a wrapper. On the paper was a pile that smelled wonderful. It was unlike any food I'd ever smelled before. I stretched my neck out and touched it with my nose—then with my tongue. It was strange but good. Inching forward on my belly, I gobbled it and then licked the wrapper until it pulled from Ellie's paws. Then licked my lips two or three times, cleaning my muzzle.

She licked her own. She'd been drooling and clearly was hungry, too, but instead of eating, she had given the food to me.

"Why did you come back—why are you helping me?" I asked her.

"My humans raised me with love and they saved me from a place where a lot of other dogs ended up dying." She rose from the ground. "You look like you could use the same kindness. If you can get up..." She nosed the air towards the way she had gone earlier. "I brought you what I could. But you must still be thirsty. There's water; a small stream to drink from not far away."

I struggled up and got my balance. Stiffly, I followed her. Soon I smelled the water just off the trail. She was at the bank of a creek that ran several feet lower than the trail. I joined her. I dipped my snout to drink and it was wonderful. I felt her move beside me to drink, too. "Where did you get that food?" I asked.

"Further along, that way..." She nose pointed the way the stream ran into the distance. "It's a human food place. Three times a day a human comes out and throws it in a big box at the edge of the big flat rock that's next to the woods." She shook water from her chin. "It's not all things that we can eat but some of it is."

I still felt lightheaded. Back at the Dogman's, I remembered once seeing a dog get free and he was so hungry he had raced up to where the Dogman lived and had torn into the round plastic containers behind it. Scattering trash everywhere. The Dogman shot him right there, no second chance; no trip to the woods and then threw his body on a fire. I focused back on her. "The humans let you do that?"

"I'm careful not to get caught... there are humans that will chase you down if they see you and if they catch you they take you away in one of the big, fast, moving things. I saw it happen twice to other dogs. I just take what's edible but don't stick around to eat it there. I carry what I can away, back to where I sleep."

She took another drink and turned to look at my shoulder, back and side, then moved her nose close to the wounds. I stiffened but didn't flinch from her; she'd proven she wasn't going to hurt me. Then I felt the water from her mouth and tongue as she cleaned the dried blood and dirt from the wound. It stung but I stood still. She got another mouthful of water and did it again. A third time and she stopped. It felt better, much, much better.

"Thank you."

She nodded her head and turned to go up the bank back to where the ground was drier. "I have a place where you can rest. You need a few days of not moving," she nosed towards my side again, "and to keep it clean. You look like a strong dog. I think you'll be okay."

Food and water had helped but I still felt weak. I thought of the little girl—the food she brought me—that's how I'd survived the Dogman or maybe it was because she was the only human that was kind to me. I had vague memories of a female dog caring for me long ago; so I knew there was kindness in animals. I'd just not experienced it in a long time, until now. I shook my head trying to clear it and looked at the other dog, Ellie. She was waiting for me.

"Okay." I followed her across the water a ways to where two huge rocks sat in the crook between two hills of tangled trees and brush that rose far above us. There was an opening at the base where the two rocks met. Inside was a space, a small cave, easily big enough for two. It was dry with a bed of leaves and a large piece of blotched and stained cloth, like a sheet but heavier and stiffer.

"I've been here for a while. This place is safe." She dragged the canvas towards the back, away from the wind that was now whistling past the opening. She nosed me towards what she had just spread out. "I found this too, to cover up with. It helps keep you warm." She turned and faced the opening, which was growing dark. The day, which already gray and overcast, was turning to dusk. "This is the beginning of when it will become very cold and soon the white stuff, what humans call snow, will fall from the sky."

She turned back to me. "Lie down. I'll tell you more after you rest."

I did with a groan; the cold water had eased the pain for a while but it was back. She tugged a corner of the canvas over me as I closed my eyes.

* * *

I woke the next morning and felt much better. I sniffed the air. There was more food in a rectangular, not very deep, box. Some of it remained in the bottom of a number of white cardboard boxes, small yellow-white pieces that had clumped together into rough ball shapes. The other food was mashed, brown stuff at the bottom of several small metal cans. Ellie lifted her snout from one and a brown lump stuck on the end of her nose. She wiped it off and into her mouth with her long pink tongue.

When she saw I was awake, she rose and came over to me. I winced as she checked the wounds she'd washed the day before.

"There's new blood but it's not coming out like it was. The edges are pulled apart on the big one across your right shoulder and along your back; I can't close them. But washing it out and not moving for a few more days will help and it will likely heal." She moved around in front of me. "Can you get up and make it to the water? If you can it will be easier to clean it there."

Stiffly, with a grunt I couldn't stop from coming, I got on my feet. It hurt but I wasn't as dizzy. I took a step. "Yes, I can make it if we go slowly."

* * *

The sun and moon came and went many times. Each day it grew cooler, then cold, but I grew stronger. And I learned from Ellie.

"Never go near it..." She nosed me to make sure I was looking where she wanted me to look. "And there are many, all around outside the woods, so stay clear of them." Ellie said. We were on our bellies on a little rise at the edge of the forest. Just below was a long stretch of flat, gray-black stone with machines of metal and glass moving quickly on it. "Those are roads," she continued. "And those things moving on it—faster than any dog could run—those are cars. Cars on the road can kill you. That's what happened to my humans. They're why I'm alone now, except for you."

* * *

The wind had howled past the opening of our cave. We were as far back from it as we could go with the canvas over us trying to get warm.

"What were your humans like?" She had mentioned them several times but only in bits and pieces; scraps of stories. They seemed much like the little girl I had known at the Dogman's. Maybe other humans loved dogs, too. I wanted to know more but I'd made Ellie sad with my question. "I'm sorry."

"It's okay." It didn't sound like that to me but she told me anyway. "They were great... I remember when they brought me home from the shelter. I was just a pup. The woman, I learned later on her name was Linda, was so sweet. She held me on her chest as we drove to their home. That night the man, his name was Thomas, slept on their couch with me curled in a blanket tucked beside him, his arm around me."

She paused to listen as a blast of wind spattered small rocks against our cave. "Soon I understood they'd given me a human name and I learned to recognize it and theirs, too. They loved me and I loved them. We were together for a very long time."

As matted and rough looking as Ellie was, I could see she was still a beautiful dog. And I could understand about humans loving her. But what about me? Even if I was cleaned up, I wasn't pretty and never would be anything but ugly. No one could or would love me, I thought as I heard Ellie's steady breathing next to me and knew she was now asleep. I was on the edge of sleep myself when I thought of the little girl. She had loved me. So maybe...

* * *

More days went by, and the time of year Ellie called winter was soon to be on us. It was bitter cold and I could see how it affected her. It seemed she moved slower each day. I worried about her but there was nothing I could do.

So we existed and survived. Ellie would tell me stories of her life with the humans that loved her and that she loved in return. I wished I could share something with her. I had tried to tell her about the Dogman and the life I'd led before meeting her but she just could not understand that a human could be so cruel. So I had no good stories to tell her. Not really. Only nightmares that came to me while I slept. But I was alive and I had Ellie as a friend and companion. It was much better than what I'd experienced with the Dogman. And life wasn't bad until that day when I heard Ellie's bark then yowl of pain. If the wind hadn't been still for a moment and I had not been outside the cave entrance, then I don't think I would have heard her.

I ran as fast as I could down the path to the creek. I heard them before I saw them... sharp cries from Ellie and the growls from what I could now see had her down by the throat. I saw the red splash of blood from the wounds on her side and flanks just as I hit the creature, knocking it off her. It was as big as Ellie, with large pointed ears that stood straight up on its head. It rolled away, but got quickly to its feet. It snarled and bared fangs that dripped Ellie's blood as it circled me. I turned, keeping it in front of me, as I backed up to stand in front of Ellie. She was still on the ground. I heard her breathing heavily but she was not moving.

The vicious animal charged me. It feinted at my throat and then reared, bringing its forelegs up. Claws sliced into the right side of my face, continuing the tear down my neck. It spun away, and then flew back at me. I got low and under its outstretched neck. Twisting up I clamped on it and lifted to smash it into the tree nearby. And I kept slamming until I heard the crunch of a broken neck and it went limp in my jaws. Casting it aside and breathing heavily, I turned to Ellie. She had bad gashes along her side and I could see her stomach had been torn open. How deeply I couldn't tell. She was bleeding heavily, mostly from the belly wound.

"Ellie..." She didn't move but I could see she was alive her eyes were wide open and watching me. "Ellie... Can you get up?" She didn't answer. A gust of wind carried ice with it. Night was falling and temperatures with it. I had to get her back to our cave. There was only one way. I got my teeth around her collar; it had been almost overgrown by fur, and pulled. She cried as I dragged her back to our cave; whimpering, when I stopped to renew my grip on the collar.

We were almost there when it snapped. I had no choice. I got a mouth full of the loose skin and fur at the base of her neck and pulled her the rest of the way. Once inside, I dragged her toward the back and went back to where her collar had dropped and picked it up. I knew it meant a lot to her.

Inside the cave, I cleaned the wounds as best as I could. The belly slash was long and deep; she still bled and I didn't know how I could stop it. I got her body across a corner of the canvas and she cried in pain as I wrapped the sheet as tight around her middle as I could pull it. I brought her water from the stream as she had done for me. She took it in and thirstily asked for more. Right after my third trip, the sky turned black and the storm hit.

* * *

The windblown snow was so heavy that for three days, I couldn't see anything outside the cave opening. Snow and ice soon piled up, nearly closing it which though worrisome, helped block the wind. If I had gone out in it, I doubt I would have been able to find my way back. I brought snow that had piled just inside in my mouth for Ellie. It helped her thirst but made her even colder. I lay next to her, hoping to warm her and tried to keep her talking when she was awake.

Though I asked for more stories about living with humans, she talked less and less. We didn't have any food and she grew weaker. The morning of the fourth day, it looked lighter outside. The storm seemed to have lessened and the sun was breaking through low clouds. The light showed how heavy the snow was around us. Piles covered the rocks and climbed up the two high points, blanketing them in white that continued up the slope of the hill behind the cave.

"Ellie... I'm going to find food." She barely moved. Her ears and muzzle twitched, I knew she heard me and I saw pain-wracked eyes blink at me from under the canvas. I touched her nose with mine, then turned and left. I looked back from the opening; she was breathing shallowly under the canvas and shaking. Please don't die, I thought as I pushed through the piles of snow around the rocks and entrance to our cave.

The drifts even around the trees were heavy and deep but I plowed through them without slowing. My chest leaving me a trail to follow now that it had stopped snowing and the wind had died down. It took me much longer than I thought it would to get there. My breath was a steady plume and I could feel my muzzle starting to ice up long before I got to the food place.

I waited where Ellie had taught me to, at the edge of gray stone where the rolling machines stopped sometimes and didn't move for a long time. Just out of sight but able to see the dumpster; she had taught me that word, too. It was a big green square thing, the biggest box I'd ever seen that smelled both good and bad.

I watched as the man with the dirty white cloth wrapped around him pulled away the two large gray barrels that he had just emptied. Their wheels left a trail of two parallel lines in the snow on the flat gray stone. As I watched from the trees, he went back inside the building with all the lights and wonderful smells. Steam rose in the cold air from vents in the roof. Once I was sure he wasn't coming back out, I moved forward, shivering so hard snow and ice fell from my fur. A wind had shaken it from the branches over me.

Carefully I crept towards the large dumpster. I hoped the lid had not come fully down, without Ellie's help I wouldn't be able to get in and out of the dumpster if it had. Thankfully, it had a fence around it and humans would have to come out of the building and be close before they knew someone or something was rummaging around. I hoped to find some good food this time. Ellie was weak with hunger and a fever; she was fading fast. If I didn't bring food back, I didn't think she would last another day.

I slipped inside the enclosure, glad that they never latched the door. Beside the overflowing dumpster was what I'd hoped to find. Riches; a flat box full of half-eaten potatoes with meat scraps and bones! I hooked my teeth in the top inside of the box and lifted. Careful not to rip the box, I found it slid easily on the snow and ice. It took even more time but I got it back to the cave without spilling any of it.

Entering the cave, I pushed the box in ahead of me. Shoving it to one side, I went to her. Ellie... Ellie? She was still under the canvas but didn't move. She was so very, very cold. I lay beside her a long time and cried. I was alone. Again.

* * *

This space—this place—was hers. I couldn't stay here and it wasn't a simple matter of dragging her body off into the woods. Just a day ago, she'd asked me to do that; to take her out into the storm... not far enough to get lost but just enough to leave her for the cold to take quickly.

"No, I won't do it," I told her

Her breathing was still shallow, with a wheezing, rattling, sound, as if she couldn't take a deep breath. "Then when you can, when the weather clears; leave me here. I'm too old. I'm not going to live." I was able to move and still felt a bone-deep chill. I felt scared. As I watched her eyes close, she coughed. "You're young... you can make it through this winter. But not if you have to take care of me, too."

"I'm not leaving you." I paced the cave for the hundredth time since the storm began. "It'll clear soon and I'll get food for us." Yet I knew that before long I'd have to try even if the weather stayed as it was. But I didn't know these woods as she did. And the storm and cold wiped the scent from everything. Forty steps from here I'd likely lose my bearings and not be able to find my way back. I wasn't scared for myself but if I got lost then Ellie would surely die alone.

But in the end, she had.

Once when we had first met she told me that after her leg healed she planned to go to the first humans she could find. It was about the same time when she had found the food place. She'd come out of the woods to see another dog. A stray like her only it must've been one from in the town since it had a cleaner coat then you could have if living in the woods. She had paused at the edge of the woods near the road; the smells held her there. She had wanted to watch the other dog and see where it was headed.

A boxy white machine had pulled up and two men jumped out. One had a long, oddly formed, stick in his hands and had raised it towards the dog. She had heard a sound and then the dog yelped and fell over. One of the men then picked up the dog to put it inside the machine. The dog hadn't moved and she thought it was dead. The man with the strange stick shouted and she had turned back to him and saw that he was pointing it at her. She'd then run deeper into the woods, opposite of the way she had come, and then angled back to her cave. She avoided humans after that.

I couldn't... wouldn't go to humans either. But I had to find another place. Even with the cold at some point, Ellie, her body would fall apart and begin to smell. At the Dogman's that had happened twice to dogs in cages near me. One was a dog that had been hurt in a fight. The Dogman was in a hurry and didn't stitch him up with a needle as he did with me. Instead, he used a metal thing he gripped in his hand; that stapler that shot small bits of wire in to hold two pieces together.

That's also what he did if the dog had little value to him. The wire bits had come loose in the night and the dog bled out. The other dog had a cough that got worse each day until he couldn't breathe and died choking. The Dogman left them in their cages for days. Their bodies had swollen up and flies and other things crawled all over them. The smell was disgusting, and hard to get out of your nose. The Dogman didn't do anything about it until he needed their cages for new dogs.

I looked over my shoulder at the cave; the one place in my life that had felt safe. It was where I had a friend by my side every day; I would have been happy there with her forever. But it was for only a little while. It seemed I could only have something good for just a short time.

I had straightened the canvas and her body, and cleaned her face, as best I could so she looked like she was sleeping. I put her collar over her neck. She had told me that the small piece of metal that was once so shiny showed her name for all humans to see.

It dangled from her collar close to her chest. She couldn't see it but had told me "I always know it's there; maybe I can't always feel it with my fur so nasty." She had hated that her coat was so tangled and thickly knotted. "But I feel it with my heart..." I had taken it to the stream, soaked it and then licked it clean as much as I could; it was some brighter and I turned it to rest face up on her. She'd like that.

"Goodbye Ellie."

* * *

I hadn't found anything as good as the cave. Hungry, I'd gone back to the food place and lay in the woods from where we, I, had watched all the other times. I waited and no one came out. I waited longer. The sun was going down and it would soon be even cooler. It was then I realized something. The wisps that Ellie told me were steam or smoke weren't coming from the top of the building and there weren't any lights on or sounds from inside. What was wrong... where had all the humans gone? I stepped from the woods, scanning the building, the road and area nearby, and then carefully went to the dumpster. There were machines, cars, moving on the road but nothing in or around the building.

Inside its enclosure, I found the dumpster was empty. Nothing in it. It was nearly dark now and getting colder. I wouldn't, couldn't, go back to the cave. But where should I go? The dumpster fence blocked most of the icy wind so I decided to stay there. I shook and shivered more than I slept.

A sound, the rumble of the machine, and a beeping sound woke me. Someone opened the enclosure gate and a minute later, I felt a jar through the metal of the dumpster. I had finally fallen asleep, my body against it, around dawn. It started to rise in the air. Startled I jumped up and backed against the fence. I now saw the machine. It was huge and I was trapped. It lifted the dumpster and backed away. I watched as it lowered it onto the flat part of a type of contraption I had never seen before. I saw the man standing beside it. His hand on two sticks, with balls at their end, mounted on the side. He pushed the right one down and the dumpster lowered. He looked at me and stopped; I looked at him and then ran. I kept going for hours with the rising sun behind me.

* * *

I had skirted along the edge of the woods all day searching for somewhere with food that I could get to without humans seeing me like the place Ellie had shown me. I'd found nothing.

The cold was numbing my paws and ears but I felt its ache most in the long scar along my back and side. That wound had healed but still hurt to be touched; the shakes passed through me again shooting pangs of pain through it. They'd started in the night and had not stopped. I couldn't stop shivering and hadn't eaten in days. When I found a small, dead, animal near a road, I ate it. It was awful, even worse than some of the things I ate at the Dogman's. But it filled my stomach. I knew I should go deeper into the woods, out of sight, but close to where I had eaten, I saw a tangle of bushes and a large rock. There was a small, partially covered, space between the rock and brush that made me think of Ellie's cave. There was just enough room for me. I crawled inside and lay down. I was tired. So tired. I'd rest just for a little while then get up and move on.

* * *

I tried to get my paws under me to stand, but the pain in my stomach... It hurt so badly and I couldn't stop trembling. I faded in and out and that's when the nightmares came. The dreams were bad; far worse than any I'd ever had with the Dogman.

Ellie was talking to me. I knew she was dead, yet I saw her and heard her voice... she sounded so very, very sad. I listened and remembered why:

"We were on vacation—that's a time when the human's don't do their jobs, the things or the place they go to most days, they can play instead—my humans and me. We were in the car—I love car rides—for a very long time. I was asleep on the back seat when I heard her, the human female, she was Linda and the man was Thomas but she called him Tommy. I was dreaming of the evenings, before I went to my bed and they to theirs, when I would hear them laughing and knew I was safe and loved. I woke when Linda screamed and everything turned upside down with a smashing crash. I was thrown through the big window in front. The one behind where the noise came from and in front of that round thing Linda or Thomas held onto when they were in that front seat. I had just a second to see that it wasn't a window anymore... it was broken, smashed in, cracked but still in place. I hit it hard and don't remember anything until I woke up on the edge of the road. My leg was hurt..." She paused to lick the long scar that curved from her rump down her left leg. It had the puckered look of a badly healed tear. I had scars like that, too.

"I dragged myself over to what looked like had been our car. Linda and Thomas were inside bleeding. He... his head was funny looking and bent at an odd angle. He didn't move. Linda twitched a hand then her arm. I crawled to her and licked her face. Please-please get up... please. I nosed her head and got it to turn towards me. One eye was gone... a long ragged piece of glass was stuck in her face. I heard her gasp and cry out. She opened the other eye. I don't think she saw me at first. Then I smelled that smell, the one when we would go to that place busy with other cars and she stuck a hose in the little hole towards the back of the car. I hated it—the smell came through the open window where I sat—it made my nose twitch and sneeze. I smelled something burning. I saw the yellow and orange flames—like in the thing that makes the warm spot back home that I loved to lay in front of— they were spreading. I tried to get to Linda out of its way.

"Oh, how my leg hurt. My head was pounding. I'd hit it hard I guess; my eyes kept clouding over and then everything got darker. I blinked and it didn't help. She screamed. The yellow and orange was on her legs and eating her clothing. She reached for me. I touched her fingers with my nose. Then I grabbed the sleeve of her jacket and pulled trying to tug her free. She screamed again. She was on fire.

I pulled and pulled but she couldn't move. Something was holding her down and I couldn't free her from it. I felt the heat now blistering my nose and burning the hair on my neck and side. Her arms burning, Linda screamed, 'Go Ellie go... run away!' I hurt so badly. I couldn't help my human; I couldn't help Linda. I ran as best I could, dragging my hind leg. I cried looking back as the flames covered her in our car. Linda! I cried. Thomas! I loved them. They gave me my name."

Ellie stopped talking and started to cry. She began to fade. Then I realized she hadn't taken a breath the whole time she was talking. It had poured out of her and when she was done, she went away. Now the fever dream gripped me; that was how Ellie was toward the end until she couldn't speak at all. She had rambled on when she was sick. She had told me that story of how she ended up on her own in these woods. She had lost her family in an accident. But she had good memories. The fun they'd had and how proud she was of her name. She had told me that we are not born knowing it; our names are given to us... hopefully by someone who loves us. The people you love that are closest to you help you learn to know who you are inside as you grow up to become what you become.

The shivers had me bad now and I couldn't stop shaking. I didn't remember doing it but I had left where I'd slept and was stumbling along a road. The place Ellie said we shouldn't go near. It didn't matter. I was going to die. No family. No one to love me, and maybe this hurt most because I knew how Ellie felt about hers. I would die without a name and no one to cry over or remember me.

* * *

"Is this animal control?" The connection wasn't very good. The woman looked at her cell phone and had only one, maybe two bars.

"Yes ma'am. How can I help you?"

"I'm over on Mt. Hamilton Road..."

"How can I help you?"

"There's a dead dog by the side of the road, on the edge of the road actually. I slowed down; then stopped to check it..." Her voice faded on the line then came back stronger.

"Ma'am, you should never do that, you-"

The woman cut him off. "Yes, I'm standing over it now." There was the sound of cars passing by very close.

"Ma'am you should not stop your car on the road like that and never touch or approach a dead animal."

"Yeah, okay. But I was wrong it's not dead. It's a dog and it just twitched."

"I'm dispatching a team now, ma'am. What's your exact location?"

"Like I said, Mt. Hamilton road, highway 130, just west of the Blue Oak Ranch Reserve. I'm just past the Grandview restaurant, to the north."

* * *

NOVEMBER 3, 2006
VETERANS ADMINISTRATION HOSPITAL
SAN FRANCISCO, CALIFORNIA

She was still self-conscious about her crutches and getting around on the new leg. She wondered if she would always feel that way. Getting it to bend so she could sit or stand was a bitch. And when she did that, she felt everyone was looking at her. That seemed to always bring their attention to her face. Long pants could cover the artificial leg, but unless she did a Phantom of the Opera thing, there was no hiding the scars. People always noticed. When she looked up, they always quickly looked away. Another thing she was trying to get used to; talking to people who were clearly trying not to look at one side of her face.

Carol, her best friend since grade school, had insisted that she pick her up and go with her to the Veterans Administration hospital in San Francisco. They were as close as two sisters were. Still, that first day Hannah saw her flinch — her eyes moving quickly to look at anything but the left side of her face. She had fumbled with her purse strap and got it over her shoulder as she leaned forward to hug Hannah. It slipped and bumped against her crutch as she did. Hannah was an inch shy of average height but bending over with her crutches made her seem shorter. Carol was her opposite; a tall, classic, blonde that all the boys and some men had chased through college. Yeah, Hannah thought, she's leggy and I'm legless—well, down one anyway.

"Oh Hannah..." Tears were running down her cheeks. Hannah felt the wetness now on her own and pushed against her a bit to break the hug.

"I never wanted to be the prom queen anyway, Carol." She felt her arms still gripping her at the shoulders. "And didn't want to be a cheerleader either."

Carol pulled away and looked her square in the face — all of it. "But..."

"I still got team spirit." Hannah finished for her. They had started that their sophomore year of high school when both had tried out for the cheerleading squad and things didn't go their way. At this point they both would laugh. But not this time. Carol was still crying and Hannah was too damn close to it for her own comfort. "I need to get admitted and see what happens next here."

"Do you think you'll be out by Thanksgiving?"

Hannah shrugged her shoulders, which made her lose her grip on the left crutch. She clamped down to keep it from falling. "Don't know."

"Are your parents coming out soon?"

"Don't know." Hannah didn't want to get into that. "Have to see what happens next." She pivoted on her crutches to head to the entrance. Carol followed her to the Admissions desk, not knowing what she could say to make her friend feel better or heal faster.

8

NOVEMBER 10, 2006

THE SANTA CLARA ANIMAL SHELTER
SAN JOSE, CALIFORNIA

"How is his breathing?" The veterinarian surgeon asked the tech.

"Shallow but stable; heart rate and blood pressure are good."

"Okay," the surgeon sighed with relief. "I was worried about using Xyaline with him in the condition he's in. But I can't have him moving while I work on him. The leg damage wasn't that bad, the car must not have been going very fast. But the impact tore open some old injuries. That wound on his back and side had only rudimentary scar tissue and hadn't fully healed. It came apart at the seams like a bag dropped from a 4th floor window."

"He is pretty raggedy looking." the tech commented. "Where'd he get all those scars?"

"I don't know." She shifted the light over the table pulling it down closer to the dog on the table. "This poor boy's had a rough time of it. I'm going to get this big wound closed properly, get him cleaned up, and set his leg. Then I plan to keep him under for a few days, on an IV and antibiotics, to give his body a chance to get a jumpstart on healing."

* * *

I heard a human's voice. My head felt heavy; did the Dogman have the chains on me again? I blinked trying to clear the film that covered my eyes and shook my head. Where was I and where was Ellie?

Then I remembered; I had lain next to her cold body hoping she would get up... but she never did. She, other than the little girl, was the only friend I had ever had. The only ones that seemed to have cared about me. The only ones that gave me those few moments of being... almost happy.

I felt warm water and soft hands working soap, not the harsh stuff the Dogman used that burned my nose, into my fur. The hands were being careful around the new stitches, cuts and scrapes and old scars. I knew for sure then it wasn't the Dogman or one of his helpers. They gently pulled thorns and thistles from me and dried me with a towel that was softer than anything I had ever felt before. I hoped they'd leave me wrapped in it to sleep some more. They didn't, but replaced it with an equally soft blanket. And I slept.

I had that dream, one I'd had often, of a field where the little girl was with me playing chase. We would play that for a while, each of us never really catching the other but laughing... oh how we laughed. She had a ball that she wanted me to catch. I tried and tried, but the wind blew it away. Then I realized the girl was going away, too. But it was as if I was the one moving as she stood still, her arms stretched out to reach for me. I tried to move; tried to get back to her but kept getting farther from her. She got smaller and smaller in the distance until she was gone.

Then I woke up. This time I was able to see. I didn't recognize anything a few feet away from me. But what I was in was something I knew very well. The memory of the good feeling, just before I had slept, vanished. I was in a cage. Again.

* * *

Over time I smelled, then saw, other dogs and animals in the cages around me. There were two rows of pens with a walkway between them. I was fed more often than I had ever been in my life and at times, it seemed there was care and concern from the humans around me. But I was still locked up.

People came in; they walked up and down and looked at the other animals. I watched as they took some of the other dogs away with them. None of them looked the way the Dogman had looked and didn't act towards the animals as he had. I wondered where they went. Was it a good place? A happy place like the one I dreamed about with the little girl. I hoped that they didn't take them to the woods.

Mostly they would pass me by. Lingering only long enough to see my scars and I guess to determine what kind of dog I was. I didn't know it at first, but soon realized I was the type of dog that scared people. The kind of people who don't really know the dog and don't care to find out. That must be a human thing because I know that's not how dogs view each other.

Only once did someone pause to look closely at me. I'd seen the little girl, not like the one from the Dogman's, a dark-haired girl that had come in with a man and woman. The woman seemed nice and wanted the little girl to choose one of the animals. The man seemed impatient and aggravated at being there. He paced back and forth with his hands stuck in his pocket. He looked angry.

Duyen Nguyen

The little girl came further down the line to me. I sat quite still and watched as she stopped in front of my cage. As I had done with the other little girl, I rested my head against the wire and bars. She reached two fingers through to brush them lightly over the ridge of scars across the top of my head. I closed my eyes and remembered that was what love must feel like. To be touched so tenderly and caringly.

I heard a shout and opened my eyes. I saw the man roughly grab the girl by the arm and yank her away from my cage. The man screamed at the girl who started to cry. The woman shouted at the man, too. I couldn't help it, I thought he would hurt them. I growled and lunged—hitting the bars; the cage rattling and sliding.

I knew as soon as I did it that I had done something very, very wrong. Something changed with the humans, how they looked at me right then. Two of the keepers, workers, were there. I saw the look they exchanged and wondered what it meant. Later on, I saw it in those who fed me, changed my bandages and that had seemed to care. After the shelter was closed and all the people that didn't work there had left, I learned what those looks meant. Two men moved my cage to the back of the building; to where the public couldn't go. They left me next to the door of a little white room full of a terrible smell that came from it. It smelled of death. I had seen other dogs go to the back of the building to never come out. Likely into that room. Like the Dogman taking a dog to the woods. They never came out.

I hadn't hurt anyone. I just didn't want the little girl to be harmed. All I wanted was someone to love. I felt the pain of being misunderstood and of never being the one chosen to be loved. They covered my cage with a heavy blanket. I'm not sure if it was to hide me from others or from themselves. No one wanted to look at me. I knew I would soon die.

* * *

NOVEMBER 30, 2006
VETERANS ADMINISTRATION HOSPITAL
SAN FRANCISCO, CALIFORNIA

Her little setback with infection meant Thanksgiving in the hospital. Which was only slightly better than the year before when it was spent unconscious or on a morphine high. And the one in 2004 had been interesting. Hannah had just reported to Iraq and her first day in country she cut her chin open in a rough-and-tumble basketball game. The medic who had put a dozen stitches in her chin had told her, "No worries ma'am... no one will even notice that little scar." Hah! That was certain now.

She looked up at the orderly. "Really, I can walk—no sweat." She rapped her knuckles on the prosthetic leg.

"I'm sorry but it's hospital policy, ma'am."

The cool breeze greeted her, lifting the locks she'd carefully combed to drape across the left side of her face. He wheeled her through the exit door at the main entrance that led to the half-arc of the drop-off and pickup area and main parking lot. She patted her hair back in place wishing it would grow out faster. "There's my ride..." A red SUV pulled through and stopped. Carol and her husband Joe got out as she awkwardly stood and pulled her bag that had been hanging from the wheelchair handgrips, over her shoulder. "Thanks," she told the orderly.

"You're welcome ma'am, good luck." With a casual salute, he spun the wheelchair around and headed back inside.

Hannah felt glad to be out—done except for periodic checkups—but was very nervous. Now would be the hard part. Going back to the real world.

"Well you got the color right." She called to Joe.

"First time I ever sold a car without someone test driving." Without thinking, he tossed the keys to Hannah. She caught them but dropped her right crutch.

"Joe!" Carol gasped.

He had started forward to pick up the crutch for her. He realized he shouldn't have done that and stopped at the look on Hannah's face; thinned by what she'd gone through it tightened and became even more drawn and haggard. She slowly bent and retrieved it; then straightened getting it firmly under her right arm. "No problem..." But she felt the twinge and sting as the scar along her neck pulled taut. She glanced at Carol who still looked upset. "It's okay."

"I'm so sorry, Hannah... I..." Joe tried to take her bag. "Let me get that for you."

She ignored him and kept a grip on it as she walked towards the SUV and got in the back. She held the keys out to Joe. "San Francisco rush-hour traffic's probably not the best time for me to knock the rust off my driving. Do you mind?"

He nodded and got in on the driver's side.

She shifted her leg to rest more comfortably, hoping Joe didn't adjust his seat and pinch the prosthetic foot she'd just slid under it. She pulled the shoulder belt across her. "Sunday I'll ease back into it in the morning when there's no traffic in Santa Cruz."

9

DECEMBER 10, 2006

HANNAH'S HOUSE
SANTA CRUZ, CALIFORNIA

Hannah's phone rang and vibrated. She caught it before it shook itself off the coffee table. It was Carol again. She sighed, not wanting to, but answered. "Hi..."

"I know you probably thought about not picking up the phone. Didn't you?"

"Yep, you know me so well." She wasn't mad at her and Carol knew that. She just didn't want to talk. Carol knew that, too. "I answered because you mean well." And she did. Carol had always been a fixer of things, mostly her friends with problems. Hannah had been one of her projects on and off again over the 25 years they had been best friends. It seemed she had become a full-time project for Carol since she had come home from the hospital.

"You doing okay?" Not waiting for an answer she added. "Hannah, I'm worried about you."

"I'm fine, everything's fine."

"I haven't heard from you since a couple of days after you got home from the VA hospital." There was more than a hint of an accusation in her tone. "The morning your parents left."

"Well, I wasn't at my best that day." It had been a long time since any of her days would be considered good much less best. And that morning she had argued with her father. Not the worst day of her life by far but still not a very good one.

"They just wanted to help you Hannah. Why didn't you let your mom stay with you for a while?"

"Because she drives me up the wall, Carol. You know that. She always has. At Walter Reed, then back here and all of the first day I was out of the VA hospital, she looked at me as if I was a broken doll she needed to mend. I don't need that." Hannah looked at her watch, figuring she would give her two more minutes.

"She loves you, Hannah."

"I know that but her way doesn't work for me."

"She means well, and you could have let your dad handle her. He offered to stay, too."

"Yeah... there's a lot of that going around. And dad couldn't take more time off without getting in deep shit with his boss. He's already spent enough time, since I arrived at Walter Reed from Ramstein, dealing with what's happened to me."

"Have you talked to him since your fight?" Carol had had a ring-side seat for it and heard the last thing he'd said, leaning out of the rental car window before he backed out of Hannah's driveway:

"I'm tired of the sniping back and forth, Hannah. Maybe you'll never fly again but you can't let some guy who pulled the trigger on an RPG decide the rest of your life. Don't sit around and feel sorry for yourself. That's going to dishonor those you served with, the man that died beside you, and those who worked to save your life. Most importantly, you're better than this... you're my daughter and I love you. But you act like you're under sod at Arlington National Cemetery or wish you were." He had shaken his head with that hard look on his face as he stared at her. "Don't pass up the second chance you've been given."

Hannah's conscience twinged with guilt at Carol's question. "No I haven't... but I will soon. I'm kind of tired Carol, what's up?

"I'm volunteering at an animal shelter over in San Jose. They have a new program for wounded veterans. I think it would be good for you and might help."

Hannah answered her without listening to what she had said. "I'm fine Carol... really." She looked at her watch. It was past time. "Listen, I don't have time right now; I really have to g-"

She cut her off. "Dammit, Hannah! Don't pull that shitty trick of yours on me."

That made her reconsider bailing out on the call. "You never curse. You used to tell everyone that's why I was your best friend; I'd handle that for you." She paused. "What shitty trick?"

"The, I have to go now, thing you pull when you don't want to be confronted on anything. You run away. And you're a stubborn... a stubborn... a stubborn..."

"A stubborn what?"

Carol took a deep breath. "Shithead... you're a shithead."

Hannah snorted. "You know even with one leg I can still kick your ass."

"True." Carol laughed. "But you'll likely fall down and then who'd help you up?"

It struck Hannah how much she loved her friend and how much Carol loved her. "You will."

"That's right..." Carol's toughness peeled away and Hannah heard the catch in her voice. She took a deep breath, closed her eyes and realized she had to hear her out. She owed her that and much more.

"Okay, what is that you want to talk about?"

"So there's this program to match up wounded veterans with a dog, a companion. And-"

Despite her good intentions, Hannah cut her off. "We talked about this before. You know I don't like animals. I've never had a pet. Never wanted one."

"Yes. And you used to be the girl who wasn't afraid to take on anything or anyone, who did everything and went everywhere; always on the go."

"I've grown up Carol. I'm not that girl anymore. I'm not the same."

"Bullshit. You're hiding like a coward."

Hannah blinked at that and started to bristle. This was not the normal Carol but that didn't matter. "Listen..."

"No. You listen, Hannah. You lost a leg. Okay. That's terrible but that's not an excuse or reason to lose a life... to stop being who you are."

Pain and anger mixed in her voice. "Have you looked, I mean really looked, at my face? Don't answer. I know you did because I saw you flinch that first day you saw me. You still have trouble looking at me. I might as well put a bolt through my neck and call me Frankenstein."

"You never were pretty—so you claimed."

"What!" Hannah couldn't believe Carol had said that. She started to get mad. Then she realized Carol was right. She felt she wasn't pretty—the model beauty—a California girl type like her and the others she had grown up with; and she had always admitted it taking pride instead in being athletic and outgoing. She hadn't minded being different from her friends. But she also hadn't been ugly like she was now.

Carol spoke in a rush of words. "You've never been vain or gave a damn about being what other people thought was beautiful. Why are you so concerned now?"

"What do you want Carol?" Hannah felt a wave of fatigue come over her. She just wanted to lie down.

"I want you to live and to realize there's so much to be thankful for because you are alive. I want you to be... you."

"I'm not that Hannah anymore." She felt her hand start to shake and held the phone in both hands. "I'm not her." She whispered.

She could hear the tears in Carol's voice. "Not on the outside. You're right. And never will be again. And some of what's inside you has changed, too. How could it not? But deep inside, where it counts most, you are still the same, just like your dad said. You just have to find that you're still in there... and it's okay to come out."

Hannah sighed. "What do you want me to do?"

"Come with me or meet me there at the shelter tomorrow morning." She paused as if expecting a protest. "I'll email you the address."

10

DECEMBER 11, 2006

SANTA CLARA ANIMA SHELTER

SAN JOSE, CALIFORNIA

SHE WAS GLAD NO ONE WAS IN THE PARKING LOT. Hannah felt embarrassed at her awkwardness. It was still difficult to swing her left leg—what had become her left leg—out and plant it to get out of the SUV and stand.

Carol was hurrying towards her through the parking lot. Moving like someone barefooted on hot summer asphalt, trying to get to a cool patch of grass. Only it was December, an uncommonly cold one—there'd already been a lot of snow, damn near a blizzard, to the east, and there were patches of black ice in the parking lot.

Hannah muttered. "I'll be lucky if I don't bust my ass."

"Hannah, let me..." Carol called out. She always wanted to help, Hannah smiled. But it had a unpleasant taste to it; that of too much of a good thing.

"Buy me a drink? Sure, but maybe later okay? It's still early." Hannah quipped back, ignoring the soreness in her stump and the ache in her other leg from bearing her weight unequally. She started moving and picked up speed to meet Carol instead of waiting for a hand; help she still resented and then always regretted feeling that way. The doctors, nurses, friends and even well-wishing strangers hadn't been the ones that launched the RPG that took her Apache out; killing her copilot and shearing off her leg not to mention the damage done to her arm, face, and left ear.

"How are you?" Carol reached for her arm but Hannah met it with a handshake.

"Fine, I'm fine." She could see Carol wasn't buying that but let it go.

She stayed at Hannah's side, matching her slower pace, and just before reaching the entrance moved ahead to open the door for her.

"Thanks." It sounded a bit strained even to her.

Carol had followed her in and stepped to the counter. "Hi Janice," she told the teenager with the braces who was entering something into a computer. "We're going in back." The girl barely nodded but reached in front of her to press a button to release the door with a buzz as Carol pulled it open.

Hannah followed her without paying attention. She had heard from other veterans about how much having a pet, especially a dog, had helped them heal. She wasn't much of an animal lover. Though she wouldn't—couldn't—admit it; she desperately needed something or someone that would help her cope. She had backed off her pain meds; she knew others that had gone down that rabbit hole to never return—and lain awake most of the night thinking about the need for them and for anything to stop the nightmares.

"What was that Carol?" She had said something she'd missed.

"Cat or dog?"

They had gone through a small office area and were now standing in front of two doors; over the one on the right was a picture of a black cat. Over the left was a puppy with a chew bone. She walked towards that one.

"Dog it is!

Hannah wondered how Carol could always sound so damned happy; on any day and at any time. She even sounded over the phone as if she had a smile on her face and a song in her heart. Except for that phone call late yesterday. She stepped through the door Carol held for her and saw a forty, maybe fifty, foot deep room. It had a concrete floor with two rows of pens that ran along the walls. It made her think of a military prison she'd seen once with an Army buddy who was in the Military Police. Walking down the center, she passed the cute, the furry, and the cuddly; looking in at each but none of them made an impression with her.

They were near the end of the rows, close to what looked like a storage area. She peeked in and saw the large roll-up door, for a dock, at the far end. Just past that was a small room and across from it, on the far wall, was a double set of doors. She walked into the area and then turned back. This was the end and she hadn't seen anything to draw her interest. Hannah was both relieved and a little sad. Glad she had done what Carol asked; maybe now she'd back off a bit. She was just doing this to make Carol feel better and was about to claim she had a doctor's appointment back in Santa Cruz. That was her automatic escape for bailing out on anything that was uncomfortable, anything that meant being around people longer than she had to.

But she realized an unexpected feeling had come over her. Part of her wanted what Carol wanted for her, what she had hoped for. To find another living creature to be with so she wouldn't be so damn lonely. Someone she didn't need to be scared about what thoughts went through their head when looking at her. Someone who wouldn't judge or ask questions she didn't want to answer. Here she stood and it hadn't happened; she hadn't found anyone. The desire for that, that she hadn't acknowledged until now, was strong. And she was so weak. She started to tell Carol she was leaving.

As she did, she heard a rustling sound of something moving behind her. She turned towards the sound and noticed one cage set back from the rest, draped with a dark blanket. It sat next to the door into the small room.

"What's this?" Something inside moved. The cage shifted a bit.

"Oh." Carol did not sound happy. "That's death row," she said sadly. "Dogs they can't place with someone, for one reason of the other. This is where they..." She gestured at the room.

Carol stepped closer to it and got a whiff of chemicals and cleansers. Turning and awkwardly bending, she lifted the blanket and looked closer at what was in the cage. The dog inside was white and black. Something about it looked different. She pulled the blanket completely off and the dog blinked under the harsh lights.

Now she could see he was covered with scars. Those on the right side of his face were almost like hers. Unconsciously her hand rose to trace the line of them from temple to chin on her face. She leaned down and looked closer at his body scars and the long ragged one that ran along his back and down his side all the way to the base of his hip. The fur along it had been shaved and was just now growing back. She saw the pink puckers where dozens, maybe hundreds, of stitches had held the massive wound closed. She ran her hand down her side past the hip to mid-thigh where her artificial leg began. Awkwardly, she manipulated the leg so she could kneel using the cane for support. He looked up at her. In his eyes, she saw how lonely, scarred, and scared he was. His eyes told her he had been hurt more inside than out. She knew that look. She saw it in the mirror each morning.

"What happened to him?"

"He was found over near the reserve, nearly dead. Someone called in that they'd found a dead dog. A car had hit him, damaged his leg but he had other, older injuries, too, and some kind of infection. Animal Control thought he was a goner when they got there. They realized he wasn't dead and brought him to our emergency veterinarian."

"Did he get all those scars from wild animals in the woods?"

"We don't know." Carol shook her head and her stance and body language showed she'd rather not be around this end of the building and anywhere near this dog.

"What's his name?"

"We haven't given him one. With his kind... you know... we usually don't."

Hannah looked up at Carol. "His kind?"

"You know, pit bulls. They're dangerous."

Hannah looked at the way he cocked his head and watched her. His square face and big, clear, brown eyes made her think of Mike, her co-pilot back in Iraq. She knew the dog was studying her just as she was he; and something clicked. She was certain. "I'll call him Chief."

"What!" Carol was alarmed. "You can't, Hannah!" Her voice actually squeaked when she said it.

She'd never heard her friend worked up like that. "Why not? You wanted me to pick a pet. I have."

"He could be, probably is, dangerous!" Carol looked at the dog as if he was about to break out and attack them. "You can't trust him, Hannah."

"I'll sign whatever waiver you need me to. I want to take him home with me today." She reached her fingers through the mesh, barely hearing Carol's gasp behind her. "You want to go home with me, boy?" The dog edged towards her, craning his neck closer he sniffed, and then licked her fingers. Over them, his eyes cast up and met hers. She nodded and it seemed, to her, his head bobbed up and down a bit. "See... he likes me."

* * *

I saw her, the woman who pulled the cover from my cage; kneel down but not like other humans. Something flashed across her face. It came and went quickly but haunted her eyes. I've seen that look in the eyes of dogs in pain; the ones at the edge. Scared of what might be next. I'd never seen that in the handful of humans I'd been around though. Before kneeling, she'd rubbed her hip and leg. Was she hurt there?

She wasn't comfortable on the floor by my cage. She bared her teeth, the skin pulling tight around them, as she knelt but it was for just a second; again, it looked like she was in pain. I'd seen women dog owners at the Dogman's fights. Was she one? Would she be the one to take me in the room and kill me or out to the woods to do it there?

She said something to the other human—the tall one—who wouldn't come close to me. She was shaking her head. I knew from the little girl, the Dogman's daughter. That meant no. No what?

The woman still had her fingers in my cage. Only the little girl had done that. I leaned towards her, checking her scent and for any sign of danger. I scanned her other hand to make sure it wasn't coming in low or to the side with a prod—the kind that didn't make me bleed but sparked and brought me down in a puddle of my own pee. No. That hand still had a white knuckle grip on that vertical stick she had her weight on.

I edged closer to her fingers and stretched my nose towards them; nearly touching. They didn't jerk away or grab at me. They were steady. I hesitantly licked them. I heard her say something and watched closely to see what would happen next.

The woman's head turned to the other woman. The tall one was shaking her head as she walked away. The woman beside my cage shifted but didn't remove her fingers. I moved closer to her. I could tell she was tense but that she wouldn't hurt me. Cruelty has an odor that clings. The Dogman had it; some of his helpers, too. Only the little girl I had met smelled different; she didn't have that stench. This woman was like that. Her fingers curled and she brushed them along the side of my head. I closed my eyes and lowered my head to the ground, lying flat with my paws under my chin. She pulled her hand out to reach in again lower; her fingers light on the top of my head. Eyes closed I lay there quietly wondering what was going to happen.

I felt the cage shift and opened my eyes. The woman gripped one corner and, using it and the stick to help, stood and faced the tall woman who'd returned. With her was a woman I'd seen before; the other humans around seemed to do what she wanted. She must be the leader and had followed the two workers when they'd moved my cage back here. She had stood there a while looking at me and then covered my cage with the blanket. One of the men who had helped her was there too. The one who always wore the long things on his hands and arms just like the Dogman used when training a dog.

The first time I saw him I hadn't wanted to come out. He reached in to click a leash on me and I let him. I heard him talking, but didn't understand. Not like with the little girl; after a while, I knew exactly what she meant when she would visit and talk to me.

He hadn't moved fast. I had slowly come out of the cage and he had clicked the leash on me and briefly rested his hand on my head. He had led me through the back of the building to a side door that opened to a large fenced in area with a patch of grass under a tree. The man then began to trot and I matched him. We did this for a while and then he let me do my business by the tree. I sniffed the breeze. It was strange and wonderful; much better than the old blanket and metal smell and the stink of too many animals in a too small space. I had looked up at him, panting, and he smiled. Every day he had done this with me. Was it that time for today?

A leash was in his hand now so I thought it must be. He turned to the short woman with the scarred face. She was doing something with the leader. Her hand was moving over some papers pinned to a board the leader had given her. She handed it back and the leader said something to the scarred woman. She straightened and leaned towards the leader. Her voice was sharp with a snap to it. Maybe she, the scarred one, was the real alpha female. The one who I had thought was the leader took a step back.

The scarred woman turned and gestured at the man. He opened my cage. I lay still as he knelt and clicked the leash to my collar. He stood and backed away from the cage, taking up the slack in the leash. When it was taut, I got up and took a hesitant step out. I looked at the man and then the woman who had knelt by my cage. She nodded at me then turned away. The man turned to follow her. She limped towards the front of the building. When the man started walking after her, I didn't resist to the point where he'd have to pull me, but did take the full length of the leash behind him. I wasn't sure what was going on but I knew it wasn't our daily walk and run.

At a door, I'd not been through or seen before, the tall woman appeared again and opened it. They all stepped through. I hesitated, took a step, and then stopped, looking at them. The man tugged the leash lightly. I looked at him and cocked my head. Where was I going? I worried that this was some different way to take me to the woods and get rid of me. He tugged again a little firmer this time. I didn't want to fight. I don't think I had any left in me but I wanted to live. I didn't want this to happen.

I stepped out and felt the cold gray-black stone under my feet. I looked up at the bright sky and then scanned all around me. There was no fence. No forest. Just stone and things moving fast on a nearby trail; like the roads, that Ellie had taught me to avoid. Those fast moving things were dangerous. Though the air was cold, the sun on my face felt good. I looked at the short woman. She had stepped closer to me her face was turned up, too. In the sun, I saw the scars, much like mine, that ran down the side of her face and along her neck. She lowered her gaze to me and grinned.

* * *

"Is he doing okay?" Hannah asked.

Carol looked over her shoulder at the dog that was looking out the window, occasionally raising his nose to the top where it was open two or three inches to sniff the air coming through. It had made it colder in the car but Hannah had insisted; he might like feeling the air moving on his face. She knew she did when she got out of the hospital.

"He's doing fine." But Carol sounded worried that he'd come over the front seat at her. They were nearly to Santa Cruz, only ten miles and they'd be at Hannah's home.

"You didn't need to ride with me, Carol."

"Yes I did." She looked over her shoulder again. "Joe will pick me up at your house and tomorrow morning he can drop me at work and I'll get my car." She pulled at her shoulder belt for slack and turned in her seat. "Do you want me to stay the night? You know...." She looked back at the dog then at Hannah again.

"Chief and I will be fine." Hannah looked at him in the rear view mirror as he turned from the window to look forward. Out of the corner of her eye, she saw Carol shake her head.

Twenty minutes later, they pulled into Hannah's driveway and parked close to the steps leading to the front door. Since losing her leg, she and her parents, under her orders, hadn't made any concessions. No incline, no handrails; she used her cane as needed but that's all.

Carol was already out of the SUV, standing by the steps. She was learning not to offer help to Hannah and she wasn't going near that dog.

Hannah opened the passenger side back door. Chief didn't move, but watched her closely as she unhooked the buckles and snaps of the car harness. As the last one released she paused. For a moment, she flashed back to the corpsman taking the straps off her when the medevac helicopter at the Field Surgical Team loaded her for the ride to Bagram and her transfer to the 10th CASH. He'd held her hand for a moment, looked her in the eye and smiled. She rested her hand on Chief's chest and studied his face. He bent his head to lick it then looked up into her eyes. She took a deep breath. "Let's go boy..."

* * *

It was different. At the Dogman's there was always noise. In the woods with Ellie and then at that the place they'd just left... there was always sounds to worry about and be suspicious of. This place was quiet other than the sound of her, the scarred woman's, feet and stick and my nails on the stone ground. The tall woman had come in, too. She was talking to someone and holding a little box to her ear.

"Thanks Joe. See you in a little while." She folded the box in half and put it in the bag hanging from a strap over her shoulder. "Hannah?"

The scarred woman led me over to a long, low, bench with what looked like a soft covering. With a grunt, she sat down on it and then extended the leg that seemed to trouble her. Her stick was across her knees and she rubbed the palm of the hand that gripped it when she walked. It looked red, almost blistered, and obviously hurt. The leash didn't give me much choice. I sat next to her the stone cool under my tail. She looked at me and slowly, carefully, reached out and stroked my neck, feeling the long scar. The one from that man who shot me.

"Hannah..."

She turned from me to look up at the tall woman, and then looked back down at me. "I wonder if he's scared..." She ran her hand down my back and when I shifted a bit she pulled it away slowly, not as if she was scared; it felt more as if she just wanted to be careful and not hurt me. She was talking but I didn't know if it was to me or to the tall woman.

"Pain makes you wonder when it will end. And when it does what will bring it back."

From the corner of my eye, I saw her hand shake as she touched my ear. She looked back at the tall woman who had that worried look back on her face.

"I'm sorry Carol, what is it?"

"Joe's got the cage and will be here shortly." She sat down in the chair across from us. "He'll bring it in and set it up for you."

The woman next to me just nodded and didn't say anything. She just sat quietly next to me, not moving. I was tired from the last few days. I had barely slept since they moved me back by the little room. I was so scared that they'd come for me while I was sleeping. Sitting there, the scarred woman's hand on my head, I couldn't keep my eyes open.

* * *

The sound coming from another room woke me. I was still on the floor, lying there alone, the leash still attached and at my side. The noise was like a clang of metal pieces banged together; I felt a new sense of worry at its familiarity. It was the same sound I had heard when the Dogman had new dogs coming in. Or when he was packing to go to a show, or a fight, somewhere else. I lay there, head between my paws and squeezed my eyes tight shut. I didn't want to look to see what was causing the sound. I didn't want to know.

But after several minutes, I had to. One thing I knew is that bad things, the stuff that frightens you most; don't go away if you try to ignore it. I got up and moved closer to where the sound was coming from.

Now I heard voices; humans talking. At an opening into what looked like another room, I stopped and looked in.

The room was bright, had a shiny ground, and it smelled good. My mouth watered and I felt my stomach rumble. My nose followed the tantalizing smell to find where to look and I saw the scarred woman and the tall one sitting at a table with what looked like food bowls pushed to one side. They were talking while watching someone. I followed their eyes and then felt my gut clench, squeezing out thoughts of hunger.

In a far corner, next to another opening, was a man. He straightened and I could see he was very tall and thin. He saw me and froze as I stepped further into the room. I saw what he was doing. The sides of the cage weren't rusty and weathered metal like the Dogman's; this one was bright and shined like a new chain. I tensed and couldn't stop the low thrum in my throat; it wasn't a growl, but more a moan. I thought I was safe. I thought everything might be okay. I looked at the scarred woman who had pushed away from the table and was starting to rise. I looked back at the man and saw how wide his eyes were. He hadn't taken them from me and hadn't moved a step.

"It's okay Chief." The scarred woman was at my side and held out her hand to me as she awkwardly knelt. I didn't move. "He's..." She gestured at the man "Joe, a friend."

I sat down to think. Since I'd met the woman beside me, no one had shouted at me; no one had been rough with me or hit me. No one had hurt me. I decided I'd wait and see about this cage; what the man was here for and what would happen next. Seeing me sitting still beside the scarred woman he moved closer, not directly towards me but more sideways and arcing around towards the tall woman by the table. I kept a watch on him from the corner of my eye. The scarred woman was talking and I turned to her. She had something in her hand.

"Joe brought this, too. I had to make a set for you." She held up a length of some narrow, thick, fabric that had buckle and rings. It was kind of like the collar I was wearing but much cleaner; two new looking flat silver metal pieces danged from one of the rings. She held up the first piece. "This one says Chief. That's your name." She stroked the side of my face. "Chief is your name." She let that piece go and looked at the other one. "And this one says, 'Call Hannah at 555 – 123 – 8910 if you find me.'"

With the hand she'd used to gently touch my face she touched her own, the scarred side. "My name is Hannah. Hannah."

I thought that I was starting to understand about what Ellie meant when she told me her human name. The woman, her name was Hannah. She touched my chest and said that other word again.

"Chief. Your name is Chief."

She took off the collar the shelter had given me. The one in her hand seemed lighter and a different color; a light brown. She slowly put it around my neck and I heard a snap as the buckle clicked. I felt her tugging on it a bit; my head moving just a little with it. She did something with the collar and it loosened. It felt better. Then she held my head in both hands and put her face close to mine. "Your name is Chief."

Over her shoulder, I saw the tall man and woman shift; the woman making a sound as if she was leaking air. Her chair scraped on the hard floor as she stood. The scarred woman said something. "It's okay—it's okay." I didn't know if she was talking to me or to the tall woman and man.

I looked in her eyes and she in mine. I felt it then, a sense that there were humans besides the little girl that would be kind to me. That would care for me enough to give me a human name. The rumble in my throat came out without thinking but she didn't flinch. I was testing the sound of her name and mine in my own voice. She was Hannah, and my name was Chief.

She seemed to understand. Nodding her head, something I knew from the little girl that meant yes or good, she smiled at me.

* * *

The next morning I woke up and I wasn't cold. I wasn't hungry or in pain. Not new pain, anyway. I couldn't remember a day in my life when one, most often two, of the three didn't apply. There was water in a bowl and some of the round, dark nuggets of food left over in another bowl next to the water. That was different, too. I'd never experienced having food left over. It was good and crunchy. I had eaten my fill, but there was still some left. I couldn't remember that ever happening.

I nosed the bowl too hard and it clattered. I froze, afraid to move and not even sure why. I tried to move it back and it brushed against the door to the cage. The door swung open an inch. It hadn't been latched or locked. What? I sniffed it. All my life no cage door was open without a human being around.

I waited to see what would happen. It was quiet. Quieter than any place I'd ever been before. No growls, no barks or yelps of pain from other dogs in training or that were being stitched up after a fight. No wind or animal calls echoing through the woods. No rattle of cages and movement that had sounded so loud in the long narrow room where the scarred woman had found me. I could hear a jingling sound as I turned my head. Then realized it was my collar with its set of rings and two metal pieces dangling from it. I could move freely. I wasn't chained down or restrained as I had been with the Dogman. And no one was holding onto my leash, limiting my movement or making me go where they wanted me to go.

I bumped the door open wider and stepped through. The ground was clean, cool, but not cold. It was a smooth shiny surface even in the dim light, not dirt or that gray rough stone that rubbed raw spots on me. I sniffed and caught the smell of wood smoke and pine trees. But I wasn't outside. I didn't understand. Then I remembered the scarred woman. This was her home; where she lived. She had taken me from that place with the other animals. She had given me a name. Maybe she was going to let me live.

I followed the tree smell. I needed to pee but didn't think I should on the gleaming ground. I went

112

through a narrow, tall, opening into a larger space. In the corner, I saw the large tree; it went from the ground all the way, to where the room ended above us. What it was doing inside a room I had no idea; that seemed very strange. And in front of it was the woman, Hannah, on the floor beside it. She was hanging glittery balls on the lower limbs. I heard a crackling sound and turned. Along the wall something was burning! I saw branches, chunks of wood that spit and sizzled in the flames... I tensed and a low rumble came from me. Fire was bad. That's where the Dogman sometimes threw the bodies of dead dogs. At my grumble, the woman looked up at me.

"Good morning."

I knew Hannah was talking to me. There weren't any other humans around. I looked at her then at the fire. I couldn't stop another low grumble of concern. I heard more talking and turned back to her.

"It's okay; it's just a fire. It's not going to hurt you." She held her hand out to me. "Come here, boy. It's okay." She patted the ground next to her. It was rougher than the shiny floor but still smooth. It was different shades, and shapes, of stone. Where she sat, what she touched with her hand again, was a large pad or blanket on top of the stone. I slowly walked towards her, curious to see what she wanted.

"Sit here boy." Again, she patted right in front of her.

I stopped short of where she indicated. She shifted closer to me. I sat where I was.

"Did you sleep okay?"

Her voice, rising at the end, seemed to be asking something. I cocked my head and looked at her.

"Do you remember your name?" She leaned forward. "What I called you yesterday?"

Her hand came up slowly. I watched it but didn't move away. She touched my ear, stroked it softly, and then gently scratched my head with her fingertips; that spot just between and behind my ears. Pulling her hand away, she settled back next to the tree. She closed her eyes and when she opened them, she seemed sad.

I saw her hand reach behind her and bring out the stick I'd seen her with yesterday. I tensed and then relaxed as she got it planted, rose to a knee, pushed on it and stood. Something seemed wrong with her. I cocked my head as I looked her up and down. She had one leg missing. I'd never seen a human with a leg gone. A couple of dogs I'd seen—bait dogs that wouldn't or couldn't fight back—had lost legs. I wondered if she was something like a human bait dog or had lost a fight but lived. I looked up at her face seeing the web of scars again. Yes. She had been in a fight—a very bad one. The look was in her eyes.

"I bet you need to tend to some business don't you?" She hopped towards the doorway to the room I had come from. "Let's go out into the backyard." She stopped where two, wider and longer, sticks leaned against a wall near the opening into the other room. She sat her short stick against it and put the new ones under her arms. "Come on." She gestured with her hand and I followed.

On the other side of the room with the very shiny and smooth floor was a door where the man had been standing yesterday. She was already through it. Outside I smelled the breeze and saw the three trees, close together but room enough for them to grow even larger, on a stretch of grass. I trotted over to the first tree and let go. She had followed me and leaned on the closest tree. When I was done, I moved towards her, stopped a few feet away, and sat. The grass felt so good under my tail that it wouldn't stop wagging. She looked down, and releasing her grip on one of the sticks, she leaned forward and patted my head.

* * *

DECEMBER 13, 2006
THE SEABRIGHT COFFEE HOUSE
SANTA CRUZ, CALIFORNIA

"I told you at the shelter I didn't think they'd accept him." Carol was still nervous and looked down at Chief, lying by Hannah's feet. He didn't seem to mind the people around them sitting at the café on Front Street.

It was cold out but a bright beautiful morning. They sat in the center courtyard which was open air but shielded on four sides and warmer in the morning sun. Chief's nose twitched, picking up scent on the breeze twisting and swirling lightly in the courtyard, coming from the San Lorenzo River, and he smiled up at her. For a moment, she felt bad about worrying he would hurt someone, especially Hannah who had been through enough pain. But she was worried that her friend's choice of dog wasn't going to end well for either one of them.

Hannah's coffee cup clinked loudly on the table top. "Chief's a good dog. He's already learning. Right boy?"

They both leaned to look at him under the table. Hannah hadn't felt it but his head was now

116

resting on the foot of her prosthetic leg. He rolled his eyes up and twitched his ears at them.

Chief looked up at them and thought about what Ellie had told him about her owners and humans: "Animals and humans have different languages. But dogs and people come closest to understanding each other. Linda, my sweet Linda—she gave me my name—said I was a person just like her and Thomas. That's different from being just an animal. And I know she didn't mean I was human. That's silly to think or believe. But I am a person. A dog just needs love and respect for that to come out. You..." She had nosed him to make her point. "Are a person waiting to be recognized." Then Ellie had grown tired again and had lain down next to him; her eyes were closed but she kept talking to him. "You have a good heart and a beautiful soul inside." She grew quiet and slept at his side and he had thought about everything she said.

He could tell the tall woman—Carol—didn't believe anything like that. She was still scared of him though he'd not done anything to make her feel that way.

Hannah reached down and patted his head. He lowered it with a sigh and snoozed a while. It felt so good when she touched him so gently, he thought. He hoped he'd never get used to it. He thought of the Dogman and all the dogs he'd seen fight and die, how they'd not even once experienced that touch.

Hannah's voice sharpened and that made him raise his head to watch her. "I understand why they won't take him in their program. It's the same reason why you and others..." She looked at the table next to them; the three women that had kept eyeing Chief and her. "...are scared of him."

"I'm not scared." Carol gave her a look and Hannah stared her down. "Okay, a little. Mostly I'm concerned about him." She pointed at him under the table. "Can he be trusted?"

Hannah leaned to the side to look at Chief then back at Carol. "I know he can. I'll find someone to help me train him." She sat back and it was quiet for a while. Chief sensing she wanted to move to get more comfortable lifted his head. She used her good leg and foot to shift the prosthetic foot into a better position. Once she was settled, he rested his head on her real foot.

"I see how people look at me. They see this first." Hannah raised a hand to trace the largest, longest, scar on her face. Even with plastic surgery, it was a thick vine twining from temple down into the collar of her blouse. "And wonder, what happened to her." She shook her head and the pain she had been better at hiding crept out. "They don't see me, the person inside. Then maybe they realize by the way I walk now that I have an artificial leg." Hannah drank the last of her coffee. "And then maybe a light bulb goes on and they think of veterans who have come home wounded from Iraq and Afghanistan. That makes them think differently. We live in a good time. A time when our military and its veterans are appreciated; most people think we're all heroes."

She paused to think about the welcome Vietnam era veterans, she had met, received when they came home... how different things were now. "But I'm not one. This dog..." She pointed at Chief, "who lived through what gave him those scars—who knows who did it to him—and still responds to kindness and love and gives it in return. He's a hero to me." She slid the cup from her too harshly and it almost shot off the edge of the table. "They..." She looked at Carol hard to make her feel she meant her, too. "Don't give a dog like that a chance, though do they? They don't know, haven't experienced the abuse he's endured or what he's fought. They judge by appearances or what someone's told them." She shook her head and whispered it again. "They don't give dogs like him a chance."

Carol reached across the table and put her right hand on Hannah's left. "I remember the girl who grew up not caring about animals as many kids do. Pets to play with; that kind of thing. She didn't want one, didn't need one, she said. I remember a woman, not long ago, who wouldn't listen to me when I wanted her to find a pet, a companion. She got mad at me over that until I got mad at her. What happened to her... where is she now?" Carol smiled.

"She's still around, but she's not that girl... not that woman, anymore." Hannah reached down to run her palm across Chief's head, who accepted it with fierce tail wagging under the table. "She's different."

"Is she better?"

"Much better."

Carol's smile grew bigger as she raised her cup of tea. "I'll drink to that."

11

DECEMBER 15, 2006

OFFICE OF JONATHAN URCHILLAY
SANTA CRUZ, CALIFORNIA

"And you say Frank Evans at K-9 Companions sent you to me?"

Hannah leaned her cane against the filing cabinet by his desk. "Yes. I met with him to see about me and Chief," she didn't need to gesture but she did at the dog by her side, "taking their program."

"Did you hear their pitch; about what their goal is with dogs they train." A slight curl, the barest hint of a smile curved his lips as he watched her closely. "And the veterans they work with, too."

"No..." She shifted in the chair color blooming on the cheek of the clear side of her face and more blotchily on the scarred side. "I showed up with Chief

121

and they told me they couldn't—wouldn't—work with him." She was clearly mad at them, and at many things. "The man there stopped me before I left and told me, 'Call Jon U.,' and gave me your card." She had an edge to her voice.

He remembered coming back from war, 42 years before; 22 years old, blind in one eye and with a chest full of shrapnel. He knew about being pissed off at being pissed on. He leaned forward to look at the dog. The dog stared back. He saw the thick neck, bunched muscles of its shoulders and hindquarters and then the seams and puckers of the body and facial scars. He turned to her.

"Hannah, right?" She nodded. "He's a fight dog. With those scars, I'm surprised he's alive. That's why they wouldn't take him; they mostly like Labradors and Retrievers; sometimes smaller breeds. They never work with what they consider aggressive breeds—Staffordshire Terriers and Pit Bulls like this guy here. He's been a warrior and it's a challenge to train that out of them, more than they want to take on and that they want to expose themselves to."

"But it's not impossible?" She leaned to scratch behind the dog's ears who looked up at her and then at him. "To train him as the programs do with other dogs?"

He lightly tapped his eye patch with an index finger, a mannerism he had tried to stop for more than 40 years. "Difficult. Depends on the dog..." He scratched the patch. "Depends on the person with the dog, too." He watched them closely, the dog and woman's body language.

"Why did that guy, Evans, come up to me before I left, and tell me to call you?" That first flush of anger had passed. She wanted to understand her options and what could be expected.

He stood, came around the desk and sat on the edge closest to the dog. He looked down at it but the dog didn't flinch and didn't tense up. The dog turned from him and looked once at Hannah whose face softened as she grinned at it then back up at him meeting his look. The dog had been through some shit. He looked over at Hannah gauging her without seeming to; she had, too.

He nodded at her and to the dog. "Frank knows my background and experience." He rubbed his gray, bristle-cut flattop. "And I guess because I'm ornerier than any bad dog and," he smiled. "I don't believe in lost causes." He went back to his chair behind the desk. "Okay, I'm going to give you the word about what I do. Then you can decide if what I offer is what you want.

"Almost every program like Frank's and those of other organizations is dedicated to providing service canines to veterans suffering from post-traumatic stress or traumatic brain injury as a result of military service in Iraq and Afghanistan. Their goal is to give rescued dogs a new life as a companion to veterans facing physical and emotional trauma from their service to help these individuals return to civilian life with dignity and independence. Studies and practical experience has shown the benefits both sides gain from the relationships that develop between human and dog. It's irrefutable." He leaned forward to lift a folder from a stack on the left edge of his desk and placed it centered in front of him.

"Though the focus is on the recovery of the veterans, to make their life better; what I do that's closely tied to that end, is redemption and second chances for the dog, as well. But before getting deeper into that, it doesn't sound like Frank told you much about me."

"He didn't. He just gave me your name and card and suggested I call you."

"As you might have guessed," he gestured at his office that had a number of military mementos on shelves and pictures on the wall of men and women in uniform over three or four decades. "I'm a veteran. I served 28 years in the Army and retired in 1998 a Command Sergeant Major. My last duty station was at Ft. Bragg and I spent several years with various K9 units. Since I retired, I've worked with several law enforcement agencies to find and break up dog fighting operations. Mostly in the southeast since I lived in North Carolina at the time but dog fighting's popularity has spread across the United States. A few years ago, I was asked to be on an Animal Cruelty Task Force in Los Angeles to find, break up and shutdown dog fighting rings in southern California. That's what brought me close to home. More or less." He tapped his desk. "I'm from Santa Cruz originally. While in Los Angeles I liaised with a team in San Francisco and that got me back here."

He stood and paced. "For the past couple of years I've worked as a consultant with the Office of Inspector General for the United States Department of Agriculture. They're finally, at the federal level, starting to look at dog fighting and its negative impact on communities and animals. I've worked with hundreds of dogs and while in law enforcement was involved with shutting down dozens of fighting rings." He stopped in front of Chief and sat on the edge of his desk again. "Knowing that and what I do now, is why Frank told you to call me."

"So you're like the other programs then, right?" Hannah interrupted.

"Not exactly. I don't offer classes for multiple veterans and dogs as they do. I work solo, one on one, and the work is not just about teaching the vet how to live with their dog companion and the dog how to obey the veteran. There's as much or more for the veteran to learn about their life post-service and what responsibilities come with having a dog companion. It's a 90-day program; I use a mixture of boot-camp and OCS methods in it."

He took a sheet of paper from his desk covered with handwritten notes. "I checked some things when you called me. I know you're familiar with Officer Candidate School so you know the style of the drills. In the program, I show man or woman and dog how to become part of their recovery process. It's not just one or the other... they have to heal together for it to work, and for it to last. Those that I deem successful in the program I can give a certification, I'm accredited in that regard, that dogs are medical equipment and are walking medicine to help veterans suffering from Post-Traumatic Stress Disorder. I know first-hand how veterans suffer from PTSD and memories of the horrors of war. It's an invisible burden we carry for the rest of our lives. Even if we don't have physical reminders of what we've gone through." He tapped his eye-patch and extended a toe to tap her prosthetic leg.

He knelt by Chief. "And then we have dogs like this fellow. I've seen many just like him when breaking up dog fighting operations. It's sickening that anyone could put them through what they do. I hate them, the dogmen, for that. These dogs..." He patted Chief on the head and stood. "They need our help, too. He's got his own PTSD to deal with."

He took the folder from his desk and handed it to Hannah. "In that you'll find more information about me, my program and that service dogs are recognized by the United States Department of Justice Civil Rights Division, and the American Disability Act of 1990. Ninety-five percent of dogs in the programs like the one you checked out come from rescue shelters. I'm a bit different. I work with people who have adopted a fighting dog that the other programs won't accept. But when I evaluate the veteran's personal dog, I have to determine a bond has been established, and how that establishes the dog's viability to be a service dog candidate." He studied Hannah for a moment then continued.

"Once I've done that, the program starts. The first phase is basic. We focus on the skills needed to pass the AKC Canine Good Citizenship course, which is the benchmark standard in obedience for therapy dog work. In the second phase, we focus on socializing the veteran and their companion in dog friendly public places. Once you've reached a level of comfort there, we begin with veteran and dog specific training commands and discipline so both know what to expect of the other."

He paused and emptied his coffee cup, wiping his lips with a napkin from his pocket. "That part of the program is based on the common sense understanding that each of you is a person. But like with any complex relationship, we establish the right boundaries to guide us and foundation for the relationship to grow and enrich them, man or woman and dog, for years to come."

He tossed the napkin in the trash can beside his desk. "That all sounds pretty dry and lacking the reason for the program and why it's so important... so here's the thing and you might have experienced it already. I could tell you that petting a dog decreases release of cortisol and increases release of oxytocin into the bloodstream. And that decreases in cortisol lower blood pressure and facilitate relaxation, while increases in oxytocin, the same chemical released when a mother nurses her infant, gives you a sense of security and well-being. Petting a dog, being around a dog you love and have a relationship with, simply makes you feel better."

He raised a hand to the eye-patch and the web of scars that surrounded it across his cheek and brow. "If you have physical trauma to deal with, having a dog helps build confidence and bridges the gap with strangers. More often than not, their response to you shows the bond is transferable and immediate; they feel it too, to a lesser degree. But since you don't have a fluffy, foo-foo cute dog, or one of the more common companion breeds like a Labrador or a Retriever..., you're going to get push back from people who look at Chief and are afraid of him. Expect that and learn to deal with it. That, too, is part of the program."

He rose and went to the coffee maker sitting on a side table. "You want some coffee? Juice or water?"

"Water would be great."

"I've got flavored; do you like Raspberry Green Tea? That's my favorite." She nodded and he reached into the mini-fridge under the table and tossed her a Kirkland bottle. "From Costco, damn I love that place." He grinned and sat down behind his desk with his cup of coffee.

"I've found that most people adopt a shelter dog because they want to save something... save the dog. But those that connect, at the inmost emotional level, with a dog with an injury... it's mostly because they have an injury too. At a profound, mostly subconscious level, they understand they both need to heal. They fit together. And veterans often suffer alone. If they don't have physical injuries to recover from and deal with the rest of their life, they still have something pervasively damaging to contend with." He paused for a moment, deep in thought. Hannah shifted in her chair and he continued.

"The deeper damage is when they silence themselves; hide from the world, because of the stigma still attached to psychological injuries like PTSD. And that's a lonely existence filled with a seemingly endless churning inside their head. But their dog, their companion, can calm them down and get their minds off everything going on in their lives by focusing on the dog and not themselves. Then they begin to realize there is life after the injuries they've sustained." He paused to drink from his cup.

"More dry stuff you need to know. It's in there." He pointed to the folder in Hannah's hand. He stopped and leaned back in his chair. "So there you go. I want you to read what I've given you and think about what I've said." His eyes stayed on Hannah as she sat straighter.

She met his look with one of her own. "I will." She looked around his office, at the pictures and the square set of the man's shoulders sitting behind the desk. "Thanks for talking with us."

He looked at Chief then back at her. "This is an important decision." He stood with Hannah as she used her cane to lever herself up from the chair, then tucked the folder under her right arm. Chief rose with them and stood still, looking up at her until she was ready to move.

As he walked them out, he put a hand on her arm before she went down the steps to the sidewalk to the lot where she'd parked. "It does get better... life... but you have to make it so. It doesn't just happen on its own." He looked down at Chief by her side. "I think you both feel that. If you work at it, you can make things better. For both of you."

Hannah nodded. "Who helped you?"

He knew what she meant. "Give me a second." He turned and went up the steps and back into his office. He grabbed the framed picture off his desk and came back to her. He smiled, seeing she was already down the steps but she and Chief waited on the sidewalk for him. He handed it to her.

She saw it was of a young man, a corporal in uniform, with a bandage still covering half his face. Sitting at his side but looking up at him, tongue hanging from one side of its mouth, was a large German Shepherd.

"His name was Trooper... I called him Troop."

12

"Until one has loved an animal a part of one's soul remains unawakened."

--Anatole France

DECEMBER 24, 2006

HANNAH'S HOUSE
SANTA CRUZ, CALIFORNIA

I stayed by Hannah's side, careful not to make her stumble as she moved from room to room; sometimes carrying things, sometime just going from one thing to the next cleaning, dusting or straightening it.

That is except for when she took that noisy thing out of the little room in what she called the kitchen. She took the long rope, a cord I think it's called, that came from it and stuck one end in the wall. She then pushed a button and it made the most awful sound. I growled and thought it might hurt her. I moved to get between it and her, but she started rolling it around the floor. She moved it all over the floor in the room with the tree and fire and then put it back in its little space. Good. I didn't trust it... not at all.

The human, Jon, at the place we had been going to each day had not just showed me how to walk next to Hannah. I was also learning hand and voice commands. He was kind to me too, and not at all afraid like some people were when they saw me. Like the first humans to arrive that afternoon. When they came in, I sat without needing the hand gesture she made. I looked at them and saw the expression on their faces.

"Mom... Dad... this is Chief."

The man was cautious. I could see how he watched me and moved closer and slightly ahead of the female, he was with; she looked scared and worried all at once. Her face went from me to Hannah's.

"He... He doesn't look like a nice dog, Hannah. Why didn't you get a nice dog?"

"He's fine mom." I felt her hand rub my head and brush my cheek. I liked that and licked her hand. "See? He's a good boy." I recognized those two words; what they meant and smiled up at Hannah. Then I smiled for the woman, too. But she still looked worried. The man next to her spoke; his eyes on me.

"What happened to him? He's all torn up and stitched back together." He straightened to look at Hannah, a funny look on his face. "I'm sorry I didn't mea-." He stopped what he was going to say.

"I'm torn and stitched back together too." Hannah rubbed my head again. "They don't know what happened to him, other than he was hit by a car but the other scars are all older. They said those are typically associated with dogfighting. They don't know where he came from. Animal Control over in San Jose got a call about a dog's body and found him beside a road near some woods. They brought him to the animal shelter's veterinarian and she saved his life." Hannah turned left into the family room. "Carol and Joe will be dropping by. I've her to thank for Chief."

13

DECEMBER 25, 2006

HANNAH'S HOME
SANTA CRUZ CALIFORNIA

I had slept a lot since Hannah brought me to her home. I could feel my body healing. And I was learning so much; now I knew to sit and what 'down' meant. It wasn't hard. I did these things before without thinking. Now, when Hannah told me to, it pleased us both. My tail acted crazy though. Hannah laughed because sometimes I'd knock things off the low table with it. She said there wasn't any way to control it.

I still woke marveling at how quiet it was. Well, at least now. Last night it had been kind of loud — new noises coming from boxes on a shelf. Hannah had seen me looking up at them and told me. "Those are speakers and that's music were listening to... songs that humans sing."

Something in one of them had reminded me of a word Ellie had told me about that her owners listened to each year, especially when the first white stuff, what they called snow, fell. Bells, she called the things making the noise; that's what made the jingle jangle that at first had made me jump.

"They're Christmas Carols, Chief." Hannah told me. Some of the sounds worried me at first but after a while, I realized it didn't mean I had to watch for anyone trying to hurt me. I had stayed as close to Hannah as I could. We'd all eaten. Hannah fed me bits of it. "This is turkey... turkey." I'd never tasted anything like it and ate a lot of it along with the dry round stuff she called dog food. It all made me very sleepy. So I snoozed beside Hannah's chair her hand resting on my back.

A ripping, tearing, sound had roused me. I looked up and all the humans had colored boxes in front of them and were shredding them open. Noticing that I was awake, Hannah set hers down at her feet.

"Dad, can you reach that one..." She was pointing at something under the tree full of shiny balls. "No—the other—yeah, that one." He handed her an odd shaped thing. She took it and leaned down to me. "Here you go boy." It was wrapped in paper with pictures of some small animal on it. She started to tear the paper away. "Merry Christmas!"

It was big and red. I tested it. It felt chewy in my mouth and then I discovered the holes in the ends were stuffed with treats. I already knew what those were! Later, when all the humans had gone, Hannah had put it in my bed with new treats. I fell asleep with it under my paw.

And that was how my night ended. I looked down and the red rubbery thing was still there but the treats weren't. I had taken care of them quickly before I fell asleep last night. I heard a noise in the tree room. I rose and padded that way. Hannah was sitting on a cushion by the fire and next to her was another cushion… Only it wasn't flat like hers. This one had a back and sides.

"Good morning boy."

She had her coffee mug in one hand and the other rested on the funny looking cushion beside her. "Come here. Santa left this for you. Want to check it out?"

I sniffed her cup and then the new cushion thingy that she was patting with her hand. I stepped on it. It was soft. I sat on it and looked at her. I had come to know that early morning the scarring on her face was easier to see. Then at some point, each morning, she went into a little room inside her bedroom where she slept. When she came out the hair on her head was smoother and skin on her face seemed darker; the scars harder to see. But her eyes; what was in them was the same. That was what made me sure she'd never hurt me. In them, I saw love and that she wanted no part of bringing pain to anyone or anything.

She looked at me and held her hand out. This was something new. "Shake."

I didn't understand why she wanted to do it but it made her smile and that made me happy. I held my paw up so she could take it in her hand.

"There you go, good boy!"

She let go of my paw and clapped her hands. I jumped up and bumped her with my nose then rolled over.

"Belly rub time!" She softly stroked my stomach, being careful around the long scar. I gave her hand a quick lick and then since her face was close it needed a quick swipe, too. "Oooh, not in the mouth, Chief!" she laughed. "Time for breakfast... you hungry?"

I jumped up. I knew what that word meant. Breakfast meant food! I followed her to where all the food came from.

"Now I'm going to introduce you to a true pleasure. I have to do it now because my mom and dad will be by later and they think I'm crazy. But I love them."

She bent to get a metal thing from under the counter and then filled it with water. She put it on the hot thing she told me to stay away from. I sat there to watch as she went to the big silver, metal, box that held cold stuff and took a package out. The long, pinkish-reddish things I'd seen before. She called them hot dogs... I don't know why, but they tasted good. She put six of them in the water and turned a knob on the thing that got hot. I think she called it a stove. She took two cans from the counter, opened them, and spooned what was in them into a bowl she put in white, square, box on the counter. A couple of minutes later it made a beeping sound and she took the bowl out. Then she took the hot dogs out of the water. They had turned a brown-gray.

"Need to go out before we eat?" She had opened the door to the backyard so I decided to take care of some business. A couple of minutes later I came back in and she had two plates on the kitchen table. I sat down next to her. She took a plate and leaned over, sitting it on the floor next to me. It smelled delicious!

"These are chili dogs... I think you'll like them."

I nosed it. The aroma was too good to wait. I chomped and the first one was gone. A minute later, the second one was too. It was beyond good!

She leaned over chewing a mouthful of her own. "I knew you would."

* * *

It was late and time to go to bed. I went to where my cage was and it wasn't there. I heard a sound and turned around. Hannah was dragging the new cushion behind her. She slid it where the cage had been and carefully knelt, putting her arms around my neck.

"Here's your new bed, Chief. Merry Christmas!"

14

DECEMBER 31, 2006
HANNAH'S HOUSE
SANTA CRUZ, CALIFORNIA

It had been easier before the other humans showed up. But I knew, now, that this new life with Hannah meant I needed to be willing to accept that most humans weren't going to hurt me. That was certainly how it'd been since escaping the Dogman. Every human I'd met since then had tried to help me, or at least not hurt me. True, some were scared of me. But as I was learning about humans, maybe over time... maybe, they'd learn about dogs like me.

I heard Hannah come in. She was talking into one of those little squares, those boxes so many humans seemed to have up to their ears.

"No. I'm staying in tonight, Carol. Drinking, New Year's Eve crowds and a one legged woman... that's not a good combination." She lowered herself to the couch—he'd learned that's what it was called—and put her cane on the table. "You and Joe go. You need time alone; you don't need to babysit me. Okay... It's not babysitting... you're not a babysitter. Listen, I plan to drink a bottle of fine wine and watch HBO tonight. I'm good with that. That's a no hassle night for me."

I had been lying by the fireplace—I'd learned that's what it was called and that it was a good thing. It provided warmth. I'd wished, more than once, that Ellie was with me to lie beside it and watch the fire. She wouldn't be cold here and I knew she'd enjoy that. I loved watching the flames that wouldn't hurt me as long as I didn't get too close. Sometimes I had a hard time looking away from it.

"Hey buddy." Hannah was leaning on her cane near me. She shifted so she could sit beside me. It was funny but it hadn't taken long for me to understand what Hannah meant when she talked. I knew that Chief was my name, and sometimes what she had just called me, buddy and other things; they all meant Chief! I was always happy when she sat beside me and my tail twitched and swept the floor. I now knew that inside a room, a building, the ground was called the floor. I rested my head on her real leg. I had learned she didn't like it if I put it on the other one made of metal and plastic. She didn't like that leg at all.

She gently rubbed my neck and back; she was never rough. "So how about chili dogs with onions and that HBO series, Rome... You know, the one with sweaty muscle guys in tunics and leather? Sound good?"

Most of what she just said hadn't made any sense to me. But she had introduced me to chili dogs. They were great! I'd remembered the name and how I learned it eating them the first time. It was when the big tree with lights was still in the room—when her human family came to see her.

She rose, pushing hard on the cane. "Okay then, that's the plan. You and me... we'll celebrate the new year together."

* * *

JANUARY 1, 2007
HANNAH'S HOUSE
SANTA CRUZ, CALIFORNIA

Her sleep had been restless; maybe from the bottle of wine she had drunk last night. She had been dreaming of a place that she hadn't visited since coming home.

Then she woke up to the sound of someone else's snoring; something that hadn't happened since living with her hooch mate in Iraq. She looked over the edge of the bed and there was Chief; head on his paws, asleep on the rectangular rug beside the bed; the snorts flapping his lips with each puff. Sometime in the night, he'd left his bed, again; the second or third time he had done it.

She decided that later in the day she would move his bed into her room and put it next to hers. She lay there, watched him breathe and remembered waking up at Ramstein, after they had stabilized her at the hospital in Baghdad. There were so many wounded and maimed like her; most of them were from IED's. They too woke up in pain, would face that suffering, inflicted by Man on men and women, for years to come. She had read a lot about shelter and rescue dogs since bringing Chief home. A quote stuck in her mind: "Humans choose to fight. Dogs only fight because they are conditioned to by abusive people."

It was still early, gray light from a drizzly morning slanted through the window blinds. But she didn't need to turn on the night table light to see them; his scars. Just like hers, they were a part of him; and who he was now... who she was now. She knew firsthand why man fought—why and how they inflicted harm on each other. Right or wrong, they shed their blood and took the blood of others for a nation, a religion, a cause or some personal agenda important only to them. The light from the window now laced over Chief's back showing the ridge of the healed wound in the stark sunlight. How could someone do that to a dog? And why? As she watched, he rolled onto his side and his paws twitched; then with a shudder and snort, he opened his eyes. She reached over to the nightstand and turned on the light. With a jaw cracking yawn, his pink tongue curling at the end, he blinked up at her.

"Reveille, Chief. Let's eat some breakfast then go for a drive." He rolled on his belly, got his feet under him, and stood. She could see the stiffness in his hips where the scar was thickest and deep. She felt the same thing each morning as she swung her leg off the bed and slid her right foot into the slipper on the floor. For a moment, she wondered what to do with the other—the left—then stretched for her cane leaning against the wall by the headboard. She gripped it and pushed up. Once she had the cane, Chief had moved out of her way. He was now sitting and watching her from over by the door he had head bumped open in the night.

"I'm thinking bacon and eggs. How's that sound?" He cocked his head and that low oodling sound he made came from his throat. "Yeah, I thought you'd like that."

* * *

The road Hannah wanted to drive started at the Municipal Wharf. A few minutes down Westcliff Drive, she realized it hadn't changed. It was as beautiful as she remembered. It curved west along the shore for about over two miles. Halfway along it they passed the lighthouse. It had been one of her favorite spots as a kid and teenager; they would stop there on the way back. She wanted to follow the road to its end at Natural Bridges State Beach.

The fog rolling in from the ocean thickened at the beach's edge at the foot of the rocks. She thought of how she used to sit, sometimes with friends but often alone, as it came in and blanketed everything. It softened and took the edges off the surrounding stone, enveloping her in a pocket of quiet somehow not disturbed but enhanced and contrasted by the eerie echo of the gulls crying above. Then the mist would burn off and the world would come back. All would be as it had been before.

She looked over at Chief buckled into his pet harness in the front passenger seat. They both needed a place to go to and take the edge off what life had dealt them. He rode easily, watching everything, and 15 minutes later, they pulled into the parking lot.

LIGHTHOUSE FIELD STATE BEACH

She looked across the expanse of sand cluttered here and there with clumps of seaweed. She had loved the beach and water so much growing up, they all, family, teachers and friends, thought she would have gone in the Navy instead of the Army.

Looking up, she saw the reason why she made that choice. The Army, well National Guard, had given her that chance; to do something she had watched and marveled at since she was a very young girl waddling on this beach with her mother and father holding her hand.

Above her and beyond; seaward, and over the dunes behind her, gulls soared and cartwheeled through the sky. Coming into the wind from the ocean, their canted wings cupped the air to float in place; stationary in a world moving around them. It was flying and not flying; that moment when you can change wing aspect or pitch to hover, or climb away higher into the sky chasing the bottoms of clouds and then drop lower, in a graceful swoop, trailing your shadow over the ground as it raced by.

She could do that—she had done that—in a helicopter. She brushed her fingertips across her eyes. She must've caught some sand in them. She looked down. Chief sat quietly at her feet, facing into the wind, eyes bright and alert. The faded, navy blue sweater she'd given him to wear swathed him snuggly. He didn't seem to feel the cold chill of the January day. She wrapped her coat tighter, pulling the hood up more out of habit to hide her face than to shield it from the wind, and looked around. They were already at the high for the day, near 49 degrees and there were only a few locals on the beach on a blustery winter weekday.

She remembered from friends with pets that this beach, the locals called Its Beach used to be off-leash but not since the state reclaimed it from the city. She loved how it curved with views of the lighthouse and Seal Rock. She hadn't seen them in years but her mother had several pictures of her at sunset with the rock arch on one side. Just under that arch was a calm pool for water pup swims. The tidal pools, on the other side of the arch, were also cool to check out at low tide.

The park continued across the street and that's where they headed. She couldn't manage too well on sand with her fake leg. But over there were many solid paths to walk. She looked down at Chief who still faced the wind and was sniffing as if he couldn't get enough.

"You want to go check out some trails, Chief? I bet there's some good smells over there." Turning his head, the wind now catching him across the face, he smiled up at her as if to say, 'Sure... let's do it!'

"Just be patient with me since we'll probably have to stop and rest this damn thing..." She slapped her left leg where the plastic started. "It starts to hurt after a while but I'll go as far as I can so we have us an adventure." His tongue was now out and flapping in the breeze. She laughed at the sight and the sound of the gulls calling to each other on the wind.

* * *

An hour later, they had walked the eastward path to its end. On the trail, they had met a few others that glanced only briefly at her limping gait but eyed Chief and then gave him room. Stepping beyond the circular area ending the trail she slowly climbed a few steps into the brush to see what was on the other side. The ground rise, a berm, they were on descended into the back side of one of the new neighborhoods; a development she'd not seen before. Still a bit gracelessly, she lowered to the ground and sat flipping her hood back to let the wisps of the breeze touch her face. They each needed a rest. She rubbed her stump where it joined with the prosthetic. It ached and Chief wanted to sniff the grass and growth around them. Brown with the season it still carried a scent that Chief seemed fascinated by; he nosed through it as she sat and watched him.

"Thanks...." He turned to her, a light in his eyes and his tail scything the closest stalks of grass. "I needed someone who wouldn't talk. Someone who wouldn't ask things; who wouldn't look at me with pity or concern." He walked towards her and tried to climb in her lap. "Oof, you're kind of big, buddy!" He settled as close to her as he could with his front legs between hers. She leaned forward and held him. Closing her eyes she felt him breathe and the beat of his heartbeat. Both deep. Steady. Sure. His head rose higher and she felt him rest it lightly on the crown of her head.

"I needed someone just to be with me... that needed me, too." She paused and sighed opening her eyes. "I love you, Chief." He nuzzled her head with his cheek and she heard the rumble build in his throat. She knew he was saying, "I love you, too."

15

APRIL 4, 2007
HANNAH'S HOUSE
SANTA CRUZ, CALIFORNIA

"MOM." Spoon in her right hand, she clumsily held her cell phone left handed to her right ear, the one she heard best with. "I don't know... I just..."

She stopped stirring the frosting and set the bowl on the counter, taking the spoon out, which caught Chief's eye. That usually meant it was soon to come his way to lick it clean. But it didn't. He cocked his head as he watched Hannah.

"No Mom... Don't give the phone to..."

Chief tensed at the look on her face.

"Hi Dad... Yes... I know it's... Dad, I just saw you at Christmas. It was nice of you and Mom to visit. What?" Chief's ears stood up. "What do you mean it's my turn? Listen, Dad... I... I know I need to get out more. But I don't feel comfortable," she rubbed her stump, "with the thought of flying. And who would take care of Chief?"

She sat on the kitchen stool. Chief laid his head on her thigh; she scratched behind his ears and softly stroked the long scars down his neck and that arced across his shoulder.

"Bring him with me... Drive?" Her hand stopped and Chief bobbed his head under it to prod her to continue. "I don't know, Dad—Mom? What did he do, just toss you the phone? Oh... His bladder... Well, I don't know. I'll think about it... Okay? I love you Mom... Tell Dad, too. Bye."

She put her cell phone down on a splat of vanilla frosting that had landed on the counter. Picking it up again, she wiped the back clean with the rag draped over her shoulder. She put it in her pocket and hopped over to where her left leg was on the table. Chief followed her. She sat and looked at him.

"What do you think—could we do a road trip; just you and me in a car for hours?"

Chief wasn't sure what she meant but he sensed something in her voice. Her tone had a yearning quality in it... and a little bit of fear. He knew that feeling. He had it the day she had picked him up from the animal shelter and for that first month with her. Then he had realized she wasn't going to hurt him. Another month and then he knew she loved him. The fear was gone. It didn't matter what she wanted or had asked... he was with her. And he'd heard the 'car' word.

"Woof!" He rubbed his head on her arm, licked her fingers, and not just because of the frosting. He loved to ride in the car.

"Okay," she gave his nape one last scratch and then began to put her leg on. "I'll think about it..."

* * *

APRIL 11, 2007

"Can't you help me?"

Chief had watched her from the porch as she made three trips with bags from house to SUV and into its rear cargo area. With the last return trip to the house, she patted his head and scratched him under the chin.

"Thanks a lot buddy..." She went through the house making sure things were in order and then set the security alarm. After locking the door, she turned and motioned to him. She took a deep breath and let it out. "Let's go."

She got Chief in on the passenger side and hooked his harness into the seatbelt socket. Lifting the flap of the red bandanna she had bought him to wear, she wiped his chin. He always got excited and drooly when he rode in the car. "You good?" She tugged on the harness connection to make sure it was solid and checked to make sure the airbag indicator light was off.

"Woof!" He smiled and wiggled his butt to settle in the seat. It had taken him awhile to get over what Ellie had taught and told him about these machines and roads. He realized now it was all perspective. He hoped at some point they would go through that thing that washed the car. That was great fun!

She seemed a bit unsure and hesitated before shutting the door. He saw her pause, cocked his head and as he looked at Hannah his smile got even bigger. After a long moment, she smiled, too. "Okay," she nodded. "Let's ride."

16

APRIL 12, 2007
JUST OUTSIDE DENVER, COLORADO

"SAVED ME FROM ALL THOSE DAMN COMMERCIALS..." She thanked Sirius radio; the rock-n-roll channels specifically. *Dani California* by the *Red Hot Chili Peppers* had just ended as she came up on the rest area sign. Her pilot's eye and mind noted the mile marker. She needed to pee so it was perfect timing to pull in.

It was just past midnight when they reached the outer, western, part of metropolitan Denver. That lengthy stop in Zion National Park to take Chief on the Pa'rus Trail made for a long day's drive but it was worth it. Chief had loved it and was playful as a puppy the whole trail. The hike was 3.6 miles and she'd done it without strain. She felt fine, a bit sore afterwards but not even very tired. It was good to be travelling; something she'd always loved but had avoided since Iraq. Maybe she was getting her life back on track.

There weren't any other cars when she pulled into the parking area, which she gave a passing thought to as odd. But it was a weeknight. All the lights along the front row and sidewalk were out but one, so she parked underneath it. Chief was curled into a ball on the seat. She'd released his harness so he'd be more comfortable. The San Francisco 49ers blanket she'd had for years was draped over his chest and butt. I'll take him out to do his business, she thought, when I get back.

She'd been driving so long; the sense of being stopped made her feel more like she was moving than when she had been moving. Singing softly the line from Dani California that stuck in her head, "Who knew the other side of you? Who knew what others died to prove?" she eased out of the car and got to her feet. She was a little stiff from the long ride, but getting out of the SUV went smoothly thanks to the months of exercise and getting used to the prosthetic leg. She walked slowly but surely towards the restrooms.

A sharp cracking and pop came from overhead. The sound—something she hadn't heard in person since Iraq—made her shake without realizing she was. The only light went out, leaving just the fronts of the soda machines twenty feet away to offer dim illumination.

A large shadow approached from the side of the building. It came closer and she could make out the shape of a man; big, thickset shoulders, shaggy hair and beard seen in profile against the machine lights. She saw he had a belt sheath and what looked like a handgun in a holster clipped at his waist.

"You look like you need some help, lady."

"No, I'm fine." Something about him, his stance and how he looked even in the dim light signaled that this man wasn't a police or security officer. She turned away from him quickly; too quickly. She lurched on the prosthetic leg; stumbling on the edge of the sidewalk, almost falling. She tried to get back to her SUV. Shambling fast enough to make it she got one hand on the driver's side door and had it partly open when rough hands dragged her backwards pulling her towards the darkness beside and beyond the building.

"Chief!" She screamed. "Ch-" a huge, chapped, broken skinned hand clamped over her mouth.

Inside the SUV Chief reared up, getting tangled in the blanket and harness snaps. He looked where she had sat in the car. Not there. He climbed over to the driver's seat and sniffed. As he turned in the seat, he bumped the door and it swung open. He bayed, "Hannah!" and looked through the window and windshield but couldn't see her. She'd always told him when he had to stay in the car if she didn't come around to unsnap him from the seat harness and put his leash on. She hadn't told him to stay this time but he thought he should until she got back.

Where was she? He paused and then decided he couldn't stay. Something was wrong and a scent on the night air from the partly open door drew him out. He pushed it further open with his head and jumped to the pavement. Outside he could hear better; the night was still without a wind and that silence carried sound. He smelled something familiar, the perfume she wore and followed it towards the building. That's probably where she would have gone, he thought. He heard something ahead and to the left. It was the heavy breathing of humans. He saw shapes moving in the dimness and headed towards them. The trace grew stronger, and another, fouler, scent that made him think of the Dogman.

The man had Hannah nearly to the darkest side towards the back of the building, away from the parking lot, where the bushes were thickest. She felt a powerful jerk from the man and then heard his sharp hiss.

"Shit!" The man cried and let go of her. With another loud grunt, he hit the ground. Hannah saw something, a white flash and bundle of darker color that landed on his chest. She had been barely able to breathe, the man was strong and his grip had covered mouth and nose. Gasping, blood no longer pounding in her head, she heard Chief now. His deep growl was more than his usual rumbling. She knew he had come to protect her. She fumbled her cellphone out of her pocket and pressed the pre-set 911 button.

The operator answered, "911."

"I've been attacked!"

A car pulled into the rest area parking lot and in its sweep of headlights, she saw that Chief had the man down, teeth bared inches from his neck. The man's hands were in front of his face as if that would stop Chief. She saw the handgun at the man's side where he had dropped it and picked it up. Making sure a round was chambered she pointed at the man's head. "Chief, back off please." Chief looked at her over his shoulder and his face softened. His gums down and teeth covered, he backed away from the man but not very far. His eyes never left him.

She heard the 911 operator squawking and put the phone back to hear ear. "I'm on I-70, just west of Denver at a rest area... mile marker 275. A man attacked me but I'm okay. He's been subdued but please send police."

"Please stay on the line ma'am; we're routing patrol cars to you."

She thumbed the speakerphone button and lowered the phone. She kept the gun on the man who didn't move. His wide eyes never left Chief.

Minutes later, she heard sirens in the distance coming closer. The man shifted as if to get up. Chief edged closer, teeth out again. "You best lay still. My dog doesn't like men who hurt people."

* * *

She looked up at the state trooper. "I'm sorry, what was that?" Hannah was sitting on a bench next to the vending machines with Chief beside her on the grass. After the local police had cuffed and taken away the man, he'd been able to do his business.

"You never heard or read the news and warnings that were issued?" The state trooper had been the first to arrive, but had been replaced by the local police officer she had just given her statement to.

Seeing she was done with them, he had stopped to talk with her further for his own report.

"No... nothing. I listened to satellite radio for most of the drive."

"And you're going to your parents?" He looked up from his notepad. "They live in Sterling, right?"

"Yeah. Just north of it, near the state park and reservoir; about two hours' drive to go." She rose to move around and stretch. Chief stood, too.

The state trooper was looking at her stance. "You lose it..." He gestured at the prosthetic leg covered by her slacks, "in Iraq or Afghanistan?"

"Iraq." She looked at his name tag, Stockard, then up into his eyes. She'd already seen him note the scars on her face. Understanding showed on his. "You serve?" she asked him.

He nodded. "Army grunt... Two tours." He flipped his notebook shut. "Does the dog help?" He cocked his thumb at Chief who was sitting calmly at her side. He stretched a hand towards him, and then paused to glance at Hannah first.

"It's okay. He won't bite." Chief looked at the man and bobbed his head as if in agreement.

The trooper scratched Chief behind his ears and got a smile and hand lick in return. The man's square face, stoic to that point, broke into a grin. "A buddy I served with—he got shredded pretty badly—lost an arm and eye. He got a dog; just a mutt really. But that dog got him through some tough times after he got out of the hospital and came home."

Hannah's hand replaced the trooper's; Chief loved all the attention. "Yeah. He's helped me... helps me... A lot."

"Excuse me ma'am."

She and the trooper turned. It was the police officer from the Sheriff's department who had taken her statement. He pointed at Chief.

"We have to take the dog." He stepped aside and waved forward two men wearing Animal Control uniforms. They wore long gauntlets that protected hands and arms up to the elbow and carried restraints. One had a long pole with a wire loop at the end.

"What!" Hannah cried as the man with the pole extended it to try and drop the loop over Chief's head. She slapped it away. She heard the grumble and felt Chief bristle and stiffen behind her and move to her side. She felt him brush against her good leg. "Stay,

Chief. It's okay." He quieted but she didn't feel him relax.

"Ma'am..." The police officer had his hand on his sidearm. He was looking at Chief but talking to her. "You need to let them take him. It's the law." He looked at her but couldn't match her glare and looked away.

"He didn't hurt that man or anyone. There's no reason for this!"

"It's the law ma'am." He looked at the trooper whose face had darkened under a broad, chin to hat brim, thundercloud of a frown. "Adam, you know I'm right. We have to..."

The trooper took his hat off, ran a hand through sandy brown hair, then put it back on. He shook his head as he touched Hannah on the elbow. "It sucks but..." He eyeballed the police officer again who looked at him with a firm but still embarrassed look on his face. "You have to let them take your dog." He stabbed a look at the Animal Control men who shrugged and moved forward again. "I'm sorry."

"He was defending me!" Hannah cried.

"It's the law." The officer said a third time.

* * *

The drive to Sterling was nearly two hours of nonstop crying; something Hannah rarely did and never in public—not since Ramstein, the hospital in Germany. If people in other cars on the highway looked in and saw me, she thought... they would probably either slow down or speed up to put some distance between them and me.

The police wouldn't let her go with Chief. She looked at the passenger seat and instead of Chief, it now contained forms they had given her, a copy of the rudimentary incident report from the officer and his and the state trooper's business cards. She had given them all her contact information and that of her parents and had been told she would hear from them in the next couple of business days.

She was mad and scared. They had seemed so inflexible and dogmatic; which was an unfortunate word. She didn't understand how it could happen in the United States. Chief hadn't hurt anyone. If it wasn't for him, she would have been raped and probably murdered. It wasn't that long ago when being dead didn't seem such a bad option to her. But meeting Chief, having him in her life, had turned everything around. It had changed her perspective on what the future could be. The most important thing was he changed how she viewed herself. She realized that was probably the most important lesson he had taught her.

She hadn't called her mother or father. They didn't need to hear her blubbering and upset. She would explain everything when she got there and see what could be done to get Chief back.

.

APRIL 13, 2007
HANNAH'S PARENT'S HOUSE
STERLING, COLORADO

Hannah spent the first hour there going back and forth with her mother and father; each of them asking, how the police could do this. So far, they didn't have any answers.

"We'll need to get an attorney on this. That's the only way to fight it or see what can be done." She could tell her dad was mad. He was always his most quiet when he was angriest. He sat down at his desk and opened his laptop. "I'll call Henry Matthews, he's a business attorney and only handles corporate law, but he may be able to refer us to someone."

Her mother rarely had an opinion. And when she did, it was usually weakly expressed. She mostly resorted to meaningful looks to convey what she thought and was not much on taking action. Whenever it came to emergencies or taking care of things that needed to be taken care of, no matter how much of a hassle or problem it might be, it was always her father who stepped in. So she was surprised to hear her mother speak up.

"I know someone."

Her dad hadn't heard that and was going through his address book on the computer to find his lawyer friend's phone numbers. It registered on Hannah that her mother had said something. But she had spent so long, no matter how much she loved her, not taking her seriously because she was so reserved, that she didn't really listen when she did speak.

"I know someone." Her tone was firmer, something she rarely heard in her voice. Hannah looked at her. She had gotten up from the couch, where she normally sat watching the world go by, and had gone over to her father's desk. She put her hand on his shoulder. "Robert, I said I know someone. And she'd be perfect to help Hannah."

She saw her father look up and blink at her mother as if seeing her for the first time. Her parents had had their issues through the years, as many parents do. She knew that he loved her mother very much, but sometimes she didn't think there was always respect. She guessed that was part of her problem. She loved and looked up to her father so much, growing up she had thought that the way he treated her mother was the way she should, too. The last few months had taught her a lot about herself. About how wrong she was in some of her thinking. Chief had taught her even more, about how most people perceive others, and how sometimes that perception is just wrong.

"Who do you know that could help me, Mom?" Hannah walked over and stood next to her. She had taken her purse off the peg on the wall by her dad's desk, the one next to the doorway into the kitchen. She rummaged around and brought out a business card.

"I've known Connie Wilkins for 20 something years. She's a good woman, very smart, very hardheaded and stubborn." Her mother looked her in the eye and then studied her husband a long time as he bent over his laptop keyboard. Hannah could tell what she was thinking and was again surprised. She thought, she can read me and my father like a book and despite our failings still loves us with all her heart.

Her mother turned back to her. "So you'll likely either get along or hate each other. At any rate, here's her card. She's an attorney. She'll take on anything that pays. But this is something that will strike close to her heart." She held out the card but Hannah's father didn't take it from her. He kept scrolling through this contact list.

"Why is that Mom?"

"Jessica..." Her dad interrupted with that sharp sound to his voice when he was irritated. "She's going to need an attorney that has some animal rights or advocacy background. Connie Wilkins doesn't have the experience."

"Bob, I love you but you only pay attention to those things that are most important to you and animals aren't exactly it. Connie doesn't have a lot of legal experience as a practicing attorney. You're right. But she worked for years as a paralegal and as a volunteer with that group in Boulder that's sponsored by the ASPCA. And now that she is an attorney, I don't think she'll shy away from learning what she needs to do a good job for a case involving an animal. You know she doesn't have any family. She pours her heart into her work. In all my years of knowing her, she's never let me down and never let any friend down. I don't think she'll let Hannah down either."

She had rarely seen her mother actually make her point so forcefully. "I'll call her, thanks Mom." She took the card and pulled out her cell phone.

Hannah's mother smiled at her. "Now Hannah, when you meet with her you'll know when she's getting fired up and down to serious business. She puts her hands on those hips and then she's all attitude. But that's what you want, honey." She patted her on what Hannah called her ugly side; the ragged looking cheek. It was the first time she'd actually touched any of her scars. "And I know that attitude is something very, very important in order for someone to make things happen and to get through tough times."

17

APRIL 18, 2007

THE LAW OFFICES OF CONSTANCE WILKINS, ESQ.
BOULDER, COLORADO

"YOU THINK I DON'T KNOW WHAT IT'S LIKE TO FACE A CHALLENGE?" Constance Wilkins had both hands on her hips. The stance Hannah's mother had warned her about. "I'm a middle-aged black woman who paid her way through law school working as a paralegal." A petite woman in a nice but not too high-fashion dress, and red high heels that added inches to her height, she paced her small office; five steps, turn on those heels and take five steps back.

"I know. My mother has known you a long time. She says you're good people. But I can't lose him. I know I must sound pathetic... but he's like... he's like family." Hannah didn't like being open with anyone, much less someone she hardly knew, but this was not the time to worry about her own sensitivities. "He made me realize that we could both live with and beyond our scars. I can count on his love—not sympathy—unconditionally. He's all that I have that's not shared with others." She had been sitting and now stood. "I don't know if you understand what he means to me."

Constance stopped and reached for the purse on her desk. She rummaged in it and took out a pocketbook. "Did your mom tell you about my family?"

"She said you didn't have any. That you lived alone and had for years." Hannah looked puzzled.

"Wrong." Constance shook her head. "Maybe some think it's that way." She handed Hannah two pictures from the pocketbook.

Hannah looked at two dogs; a German Shepherd and a small, black, Yorkshire Terrier. Standing in front of her, Constance tapped each picture while looking her in the eye.

"That's Angie... And the little guy is Frank." She beamed just like a proud mother. "That's my boy and girl."

Hannah's worried look lessened. She almost smiled at hearing their names. "Okay. So you know what I mean."

"That I do dearie. That I do." She put the pictures back in the pocketbook and then it back in the purse. She sat at the desk and from the center drawer pulled out a legal size pad of paper, a pen, yellow and orange highlighters, and a pack of Wrigley's spearmint chewing gum. She motioned at the chair in front of her desk. "Sit down and let's get started." She unwrapped a stick of gum, popped it in her mouth, and waited for Hannah to settle into the chair. "Okay. Tell me everything from the beginning."

"The beginning? Where?"

"From when you met your dog, Chief. I have an idea. But we need to tell a story that resonates in the judge's ears and touches his heart in the right way." She snapped her gum. "But something that's not flimsy bullshit. We have to stand on some solid legal footing or it's not going to work."

* * *

ANIMAL CONTROL
DENVER, COLORADO

Caged again. I wondered what was going to happen to me this time. These human beings, the one who had tried to make me a killer... and these... the ones who put me in this cage. They think that animals don't have feelings or maybe they don't care if we do. They don't know we gave the humans we bond with, and our friends, our heart, our unconditional love.

The Dogman and others just like him abused and killed us; they made us kill our own kind in the name of sports, entertainment, gambling. They felt they had the right to abuse, torture and kill us as they saw fit. They trained us to be vicious, to fight brutally; to kill each other. They made us into something we're not.

I wanted to be back with Hannah! I hoped she was okay. I hoped that something would happen to return me to her. That's all I wanted. That's all I asked for.

18

APRIL 25, 2007
The Law Offices of Constance Wilkins, Esq.
Boulder, Colorado

"Connie, I want to know the specific laws." Hannah sat across from her desk. That's why I came over here, and to go down to Denver and see Chief."

"Okay, dearie... but I hate to read them and I'm a lawyer." Connie handed her two sheets of paper, covered with small print front and back. "These are just the one's I see as applicable, according to the sheriff's office and likely by the judge, too." She took the wrapper off a stick of gum, balled it up and tossed it on her desk. It landed next to the other three just like it. She stuck the spearmint gum in her mouth. "We have to figure out a solid argument that shows a flaw in the legal presumption."

Hannah sat back in the chair and looked at the pages. "How can they do this?" she waved the pages at Connie. "This is just like racial profiling... it's racist!"

"I agree, honey." Connie moved behind her desk and sat. The swivel chair shifted and she scooted it back to center it. "My mother's family is from Alabama and my aunt Tressie was at Selma. I used to sit with her and listen to stories about the civil rights movement. She said over and over, it's about being seen as equals... as a person with the same rights as others." She leaned forward and Hannah saw the lines tighten in her face. "We're going to convince the judge it's the same thing."

19

"I would look at a dog and when our eyes met, I realised that the dog and all creatures are my family. They're like you and me."

--Ziggy Marley

MAY 24, 2007
DISTRICT ATTORNEY'S OFFICE
DENVER, COLORADO

"You understand that this, the dog's actions, is a clear violation..." The District Attorney talked to his boss as if he was the person sitting behind the desk and in charge.

"Henry..." The man sounded as if he felt he had said that name too many times; a tired, sighing, kind

177

of sound. His retirement was only 58 days away now and it couldn't come soon enough. "She's not a local and the dog didn't hurt anyone."

"It's the law, Stanton."

"For Christ's sake she's a decorated, combat wounded veteran!"

"Then she fought for us." The district attorney stood, as he often did, to move and sweep his arms around as if he was campaigning for the other man's job, which he was. "To enforce our laws."

The man behind the desk thought, I doubt she fought for you... you priggish bastard. He knew what Henry Poindexter was after. Now that the rest area rapist had been caught, he needed a bogeyman or something to make people scared of or concerned about.

"Don't you see this dog could, maybe should, be looked at as a hero? He saved his owner's life. That right there can constitute an affirmative defense." He looked across the desk at Poindexter who was already shaking his head.

"That doesn't matter. Those pit bull dogs are dangerous. That is why we have the laws in place." He sat back, crossed his legs and looked at Stanton. "You're tired and ready to go aren't you? Time to call it a career; go put your feet up poolside somewhere." A tight smile played on his lips; it looked like condescension to the man behind the desk. "We need someone to enforce the law."

Hank Stanton was tired of dealing with him. "And that would be you, right Henry?" He hated the smug look he got in reply.

* * *

MAY 25, 2007
DISTRICT ATTORNEY'S OFFICE
DENVER, COLORADO

"Mr. Poindexter we are going to move to dismiss. There is no basis for my client's friend, Chief, to be held."

He smiled at Connie and Hannah without meaning it. The smile was the same; fixed in place as it had been in the two previous meetings over the past nearly 30 days. "You can do as you wish Ms. Wilkins but in less than two weeks we'll have our pre-trial hearing."

* * *

JUNE 5, 2007
DISTRICT COURTHOUSE
DENVER, COLORADO

THE HEARING

They had just heard the District Attorney's opening statement. It was a repeat of everything from the three meetings with him through the end of May. Hannah looked behind her. Her mother and father were there with Jon Urchillay sitting beside them. In the next row behind them were a half a dozen people with their dogs. The dark glasses on the four men and two women showed they were blind. Each wore a service branch jacket with their rank, ribbons and patches; veterans with their service dogs.

"Who are they?" She had asked Connie earlier.

"They're from a veterans group in Boulder and the local VFW, Veterans of Foreign Wars. They heard about the hearing and called me and asked if they could come and show support for you." A concerned look passed on her face. "I didn't think to ask you... you don't mind do you?"

"Not at all." Hannah gave her a brief smile that faded as she wondered what she'd do if they lost and they took Chief from her.

"Ms. Wilkins, it's your turn." The judge shuffled a stack of papers in front of him and then leaned back as she stood.

Connie came around the table to face him. "Good morning, Your Honor." She took a few steps to her right and turned towards him and the District Attorney. "What makes up the essential qualities of a person? If they consist of a being that is deeply self-aware and self-determined, capable not only of pleasure and suffering, but of anticipating the future, remembering the past and making conscious choices about their lives... then we have much to consider in this hearing." She looked around the court; a squint at the District Attorney and a smile for Hannah and the judge.

"I'm here today, on behalf of such a being... a person. Someone who doesn't want to spend his life alone in a cage. Someone that doesn't want to suffer. Someone who doesn't want to die. Someone that, despite hardships proven by the brutality he's endured, is capable of love, honor, nobility and self-sacrifice. Are those not also part of what makes a being a person? Even if that person is a dog."

Connie turned and pointed to the men, women and their dogs in the row behind Hannah's parents. "I'm sure these men and women, veterans of our armed forces, would agree that they're accompanied by more than just a dog; they're a trusted companion and members of their family." There were nods from all of them and she turned back to the judge.

"I want to be clear. I'm not saying animals are human. They are not. But though Chief can't speak our language, it is certain he doesn't want to spend his life alone in a cage. Nor does he want to die as punishment for being a breed of dog that has been misunderstood, mislabeled and vilified without cause. Others to come, to be heard in this hearing, with decades of professional experience, will speak on that point. I want to talk about the legal issue we face right now. I'm prepared to file writs of habeas corpus; and request that you consider whether this person, Chief, is being wrongfully imprisoned. We contend that he is and we believe that is provable under the law. I know the legal ground we walk today. This is not a welfare issue; it is not that we consider this situation and the possible outcome a most egregious form of animal cruelty. It's about personhood. It's about this person, Chief's, unlawful detention."

The District Attorney interrupted her. "Your Honor, may I make a point." The judge nodded. "Your reputation precedes you, counselor and I see you're going to persist with the line of argument you alluded to in our meetings." He nodded at Connie and picked up a book from the table in front of him. "This is Black's Law Dictionary. As you know, it's the most widely-used legal dictionary in the United States. Within it is the definition of 'human being' as it pertains to our laws; so all that you just said is without merit."

Connie turned to face him hands on her hips. "Your reputation precedes you too, Mr. Poindexter. And I see it's accurate. Did you not listen to what I said, now and in the meetings you referred to?" She shook her head at him.

"I am not advocating the position that Chief is a human being. But he is, by all definitions, legally and otherwise, a person; a cognitive and extraordinarily complex being. True, it's a novel legal concept; but one that is irrefutably defensible. Yet it is not a biological concept. And frankly, the biological component is not the issue. The issue is that a person, deserving of equal protection and rights, is being unlawfully detained. And before you raise the invalid argument and erroneous belief, that autonomy is the end-all be-all of the legal presumption and basis for laws protection rights of the individual..., it is not. What is the basis is the sentience of a being and their ability to suffer. Chief is a sentient being of a type that has a tradition of benefit to humans... 'Man's best friend'... you've heard of that I'm sure. It is proven, without a doubt or dispute, how dogs provide humans with something very important. It's proven that they think and they can communicate with humans, it's proven that they love and care for others of their kind and for humans, too. That cannot be denied."

"If you," she pointed at the District Attorney then turned to the judge, "Your Honor, too. If you had someone, close to you that manifested all those things, all of those human attributes we admire and cherish. And they were someone you cared for that was an integral part of your family and life... would you not protest their unlawful and wrongful imprisonment? I'm reasonably sure you would do everything you could, everything in your power; use all of your resources, to set them free. That's why we," she paused to gesture at Hannah. "Are here today. To see justice served and the right thing done."

She turned back to the District Attorney. "I will also argue the following points about the current situation and issue before us: Colorado laws violated the 'due process clause' of the Constitution and enabled the government, through its law enforcement entity, the Sheriff's Department, to unlawfully imprison Chief without due process. The Fifth Amendment to the United States Constitution provides the following:

- [N]or shall any person . . . be deprived of life, liberty, or property, without due process of law . . . .[5]

Section One of the Fourteenth Amendment to the United States Constitution also provides:

- [N]or shall any State deprive any person of life, liberty, or property, without due process of law . . . .[6]

"Note the stipulation and use of the word 'Person,' Your Honor. We also have to acknowledge this fact: Chief attacked this killer rapist in defense of his friend, Hannah Arshakunian. This is clearly an affirmative defense, which has legal precedence in courts throughout the United States. Chief's action prevented a violent crime and without doubt eliminated a threat, without harm or injury to the alleged perpetrator that could have continued to harm the citizens of your community. And this alleged perp could have possibly evaded local authorities and spread his brutality to other parts of our state and beyond its borders." She returned to the long table where Hannah was and sat down.

"Is that all for your opening statement, Ms. Wilkins?

"Yes, Your Honor."

The judge checked off something on a sheet of paper in front of him and turned to the bailiff. "Let's call..." he looked down, "Mr. Jonathan Urchillay." He watched as a solid looking man with gray-bristled short hair strode forward. "I understand Mr. Urchillay, that you have testified many times, in legal venues across the United States, as an expert witness particularly applicable to the issue before us."

Jon settled himself in the chair and scratched his eye-patch. "Yes, Your Honor. I have. Dozens of times domestically and internationally in Canada and the United Kingdom."

"Let's start with a basic question. Is this dog a threat to humans?"

Jon sat straighter and leaned forward, steepling his fingers. "I can give you one of the primary determinants used in my profession and in the Animal Control and Training industry. One of the interesting evaluations of dogs and their suitability for interaction with humans involves temperament testing. During that evaluation, a dog is subjected to a series of tests. How the dog responds shows his level of aggressiveness. In shelter situations, dogs that do not pass temperament testing will not be put up for adoption to the public. They either must be placed in special rescues designed to deal with problem dogs or be euthanized. Temperament testing is also done for dogs working to be certified as therapy or rescue dogs. Of course, any owner may choose to have their dog tested at any time. Here's what's very important and interesting about Chief's breed and it's also statistically significant; there's a lot of scientific study behind this: Pit bulls that are tested pass at a higher rate than the dog population in general. Also, and this is a fact that can be validated and verified through law enforcement and animal control databases at the municipal and statewide level across the United States. Pit bulls are not responsible for the largest number of fatal dog attacks and are not the dogs that inflict the most bites. What most people believe about them is wrong. Plain wrong."

The judge pushed his glasses further up his nose and picked up his pen. "Is that your personal or professional opinion?"

Jon gave him a tight smile. "Over the course of my professional career since leaving the Army, I've personally witnessed the rehabilitation of dozens, possibly over a hundred, pit bulls rescued from dog fighting rings. Though many needed medical treatment and rehabilitation, none of them had to be euthanized. I have been on the scene of dozens of dog fighting raids and have never come across a dog, found there, in that setting or environment, that was aggressive to humans. They were actually extremely friendly to humans, and because of their treatment and conditioning, tend to be more dog aggressive." He paused. "In fact the dogmen who breed and train these dogs will kill those that are aggressive to humans because they don't want to be bit themselves. It's brutal, but it is also how they condition the dogs to respond, in a nonviolent way, towards humans."

The District Attorney stood. "Mr. Urchillay are you saying this dog is not dangerous to humans?"

"Yes, that's exactly what I'm saying." Jon scratched his eye patch. "I've been around Chief, this dog, a great deal and not seen any signs of aggression. In fact, he shows great compassion and affection towards all humans." Jon looked at Hannah and winked. "But especially to the young lady over there."

"But this dog did attack a man didn't he? Even..." The District Attorney's tone was mildly sarcastic; he was about the same age as Hannah. "This young lady acknowledges that he did."

"That's not correct. Chief did not attack the man. He defended his friend. There is a vast difference between dogs that attack and those that defend." Jon turned to the judge. "Your Honor may I ask a question?"

The District Attorney squirmed, clearly irritated again. "Please, Your Honor... Aren't the people called before the court supposed to give us answers and not ask questions of me or the court?"

The judge looked up from his notes and over his glasses at him. "Mr. Poindexter, I believe that all sides in a hearing of this nature have a right to ask questions." He turned his head and nodded at Jon, who looked at the District Attorney.

"Mr. Poindexter, right?" He didn't wait for confirmation. "If someone you loved was attacked, and you were physically there and able to do something about it, what would you do?"

"This hearing is not about me. Our time here isn't intended as a forum for you, or anyone, to question my actions as a human being. And what you ask is not relevant to the issue at hand."

"That's not an answer. That's avoiding the question." Jon looked at the judge who nodded at the prosecutor attorney to reply.

"Please answer him Mr. Poindexter."

"I would try to defend the person being attacked. But I'm a human being and can make a clear distinction and decision that an animal can't."

"That second part is an inaccurate statement given the context."

"Context. I don't understand?" The District Attorney gave an irritated glance at the judge who didn't acknowledge it.

"Mr. Poindexter you're talking as if there's a difference between a human being and a person. As Ms. Wilkins showed in her statement, and this is something I know to be true in this situation, based on my countless interactions with human beings and dogs in intense, high risk, high threat, scenarios and real-world situations. Check my record with the Department of Defense if you don't believe I know what I'm talking about. Dogs can clearly make decisions. They respond to training; they respond to rules and regulations; they respond to boundaries. Yes; in that, they are exactly like human beings. Exactly like someone in our society. It could be a soldier or other service members, a police officer, a firefighter or any other individual capable of determining what is right and wrong and acting accordingly. Chief knew that this man, allegedly a serial killer and rapist, not only posed a threat to Hannah but in actuality, in a physical setting, clearly showed he was hurting Hannah. And he acted accordingly. He subdued the man, did not hurt or injure him though he was clearly capable and in position to do so, and responded to other humans around him without any aggression. I would guess in this hearing you'll also talk to the officers on site, at the incident, about this or enter the reports and statements into the record for consideration. Their report and testimony will substantiate what I just said."

The District Attorney stood and approached the judge's bench. "There's still the matter concerning this dangerous breed of dog, Mr. Urchillay and the law governing the issue before us. That the law protects humans from dogs that have proven to be dangerous and untrustworthy." With a glance at Jon, he turned back to his table and sat down.

Jon shook his head. "Your Honor, clearly Mr. Poindexter did not listen to me. I've worked with hundreds of dogs like Chief." He tapped his eye-patch and rubbed his chest as he leaned forward. "But it was a human that took my eye and nearly killed me." He looked at Hannah. "It was a dog that helped save me."

"Are you done, Mr. Poindexter?" the judge asked. The District Attorney nodded. "You may step down Mr. Urchillay." He made a check mark on his list. "Let's have Ms. Hannah Arshakunian now."

Hannah rose and stiffly moved to the stand. She had barely seated herself and leaned her cane against the railing when the District Attorney was in front of her.

"How long have you owned the dog?" He asked Hannah.

"My friend's name is Chief."

"Excuse me?" The District Attorney sounded confused and a little irritated at not being answered.

"My friend's name is Chief."

"That's not relevant. How long have you owned the dog?"

Her voice sharpened. It was the tone of an army officer and assault helicopter pilot that demanded you had damn well better listen to and respect her. "It's very relevant."

"Your Honor, please direct her to answer my questions."

Hannah turned to speak calmly to the judge. "Your Honor, I'll answer any question that's appropriate and asked of me correctly."

The judge pushed his glasses up his nose and looked down it at her. "What's wrong with the question?"

"His tone was disparaging and his question was inaccurate."

"Your Honor..." Pompous bluster crept into the District Attorney's tone. "We really don't have time for this."

The biting edge came back into Hannah's voice. "Really? There's a life at stake here. Shouldn't we take the time required to arrive at the truth and render fair judgment?"

"Your Honor, I insist..." The District Attorney squawked.

There was a hint of a smile showing on the judge's lips as he commented before the District Attorney could jump on what she had said. "Truth and fairness is what's expected and that's why we're here. But I fail to see your point regarding the question he asked you." The judge held his hand up. "I've listened to quite a lot in this hearing that's food for thought." He turned to Hannah. "But again, what's your point about whether you are owner of the dog?"

She looked at the District Attorney who was biting his lip as she responded to the judge. "It implies that someone I acknowledge as a friend and loved member of my family is an object. He's not. He shares his life with me as I do with him. He is a very dear friend. I don't own him."

"Your honor, please..." The District Attorney's voice dripped with insincerity. "I understand how people feel about their pets. But this is a dangerous animal. She is its owner."

"Your Honor, I don't own my friend. I adopted him, brought him into my home and into my life, yes. But own him. No."

"Did you pay for its licensing?" The District Attorney asked her.

"Yes."

"Doesn't licensing imply and, arguably, legally establish ownership?"

"Let me ask you this. You're an attorney, correct?" Hannah asked him.

He turned to the judge with a sour look on his face. "Your Honor, please!"

The judge pushed his glasses up then looked down his nose at the man. "I'm curious to hear where this is headed." He nodded at Hannah then looked at the District Attorney. "Answer the lady's question."

The sourness didn't fade. "Yes, I'm an attorney." He folded his arms across his chest.

"Are you licensed to practice law?"

He looked at the judge who returned the look without comment.

"Yes, I'm licensed."

"Who are you licensed with or through, what organization or regulatory body?"

"I can't believe this..." He looked at the judge who again stared back without comment.

"The Colorado Bar." He sniffed then added, "And Utah, and New Mexico."

"Do any, or all of them, own you or any piece of you?"

"No. Your Honor this is gone too far. Can we get down to the business at hand? This animal..."

"Your Honor!" Hannah's voice rang out. "My point is that my friend, Chief, is being unlawfully detained. He is a person deserving of equal rights and protection under our laws. As you've heard in this hearing, my friend has not harmed anyone. In fact, were it not for him I would likely be dead. He has saved my life more than once I believe... and if he hadn't acted in my defense; your city would still have a serial killer and rapist out there on your streets. A threat to the citizens who elected you and whose taxes pay your salaries."

The judge headed the District Attorney off. "Well, she does have certain facts correct. Can't argue against that." He held up his hand to stop the District Attorney's complaint. "In the opening you cited the law and its applicability. It's my job to sift through circumstances and the facts, to determine what's right." He looked at Hannah. "And arrive at what this young lady stated so clearly... truth and fairness." He settled his glasses again, looked down at a sheet of paper in his hand, and then up again at the District Attorney. "Unless you have some questions, the answers of which directly pertain to the law and your belief in its applicability, we are going to move on."

"Your Honor; the law is the law!"

"Yes, so it is. And truth and what's right are subject to sound interpretation of our laws. Do you have any questions that are truly germane to the issue before us? No? Then let's proceed." He gave Hannah a tight smile. "Ma'am you may step down. Let's take a short, ten minute, recess and then have state trooper Adam Stockard up here."

* * *

"You were the first police officer on the scene where you not?"

"I was." Adam Stockard looked even larger within the confines of the witness stand.

"When you arrived what was the situation?"

"Ms. Arshakunian had been attacked by a man that state and local authorities believe is now responsible for six other attacks in the Denver metropolitan area. When I arrived on the scene, the man was down and had been restrained by Ms. Arshakunian, holding his own gun on him." The trooper paused as he struggled to stop his grin. "The dog, Chief, was sitting next to the man's head with Ms. Arshakunian by his side. Given the situation, both of them were calm and collected. The man however kept shouting; concerned about the dog being so close to his face."

"And you took a statement from her where she acknowledged that her dog attacked the man?"

Adam's eyes narrowed at the District Attorney. "In her statement, Ms. Arshakunian, described that she called out for help and Chief responded; defending her and subduing the man. From a law enforcement perspective, I saw no indications that the man was harmed by Chief or that the dog was acting aggressively. His response was clearly defensive."

"Trooper Stockard, please limit your responses to the question asked."

"I also patted Chief on the head and he licked my hand. Clearly he respects humans that deserve it."

Angered, the District Attorney pleaded to the judge. "Your Honor!"

Ignoring him, the judge leaned forward towards Adam. "I have a question. What's the status of the investigation and prosecution of this alleged serial rapist and killer?" He sat back; ignoring the District Attorney who was now squirming like a boy denied permission to go to the bathroom.

"Your Honor, you can get more details from the investigating officers both state and local. But I've been informed that they found clear evidence, including DNA that will prove without a doubt that the man Chief subdued is responsible for the rape and murder of at least six women whose bodies have been found in the past few months in this area."

The judge nodded and made a couple of notes on his pad of paper. "Any other questions of this officer, Mr. Poindexter?"

The District Attorney, clearly still affronted, gave him a curt shake of his head.

"Good. We'll break for lunch, one hour, and then hear closing statements."

* * *

"Thank you Mr. Poindexter." The judge said. "I understand fully your position."

The district attorney snidely corrected him. "It's the law, and therefore the city and state's position, your honor."

"Yes..." The judge raised his eyebrows and replied dryly. "Okay, Ms. Wilkins, it's your turn."

Connie rose and came around in front of the table but didn't approach the bench. "Your Honor my client has asked me if she could present her own closing statement. If you'll allow her."

The judge nodded. "Ms. Arshakunian."

Hannah was more nervous than she had ever been in her life. What she said next or didn't may result in Chief losing his life. She pressed her palms flat on the table top and pushed up to stand. She picked up her cane and started to move from her chair — then held it — horizontally in both hands her head down looking at it. After her third deep breath, she heard the District Attorney tapping on his table. No doubt with that expensive pen with the white nib he carried in his shirt pocket and flourished in their meetings before the hearing.

"Ms. Arshakunian, are you okay?" The judge asked leaning forward.

She looked behind at her parents then turned to face the judge. "Yes sir... Yes, Your Honor." She set the cane on the table and slowly, a bit shakily, limped towards him. She was tired and her stump hurt. The foot she no longer had itched and ached terribly. She took another deep breath.

"In war it's unfortunate that innocents die... and one of the first casualties, for young people like me, is our own innocence. We see and sometimes do terrible things because duty calls for it. It's war. We use that as a reason. As an excuse. But that doesn't make it any easier to bear. I volunteered. I chose to serve our country. What happened to me is as much my responsibility as the insurgents that pulled the trigger."

She turned to look at her father. "My responsibility." His face was white and a tear trickled down his cheek. "I know..." She looked at the District Attorney and then the judge. "You're thinking, how is this relevant." She knew when she sweated because she felt its trail down the funnel of the largest scar on her face and neck. She touched a hand to cheek and her fingertips came away damp. She was sure it was sweat.

"We decorate with medals, and venerate, our servicemen and women who in battle risk their own lives to save others." She blinked. She was sure it was sweat in her eyes. "Firefighters and police officers, too. My friend..." She looked at the District Attorney who shifted in his chair. "Is a person that proved his love for me at his own risk despite having been terribly hurt and brutalized by humans in his past. You've seen Jon Urchilay's report and his notes on Chief's likely background. Despite what happened to him at the hands of humans, Chief recognized that not all of us are like that— the breed that did such harm to him— and he didn't hesitate to come to my aid.

"So I'll leave you with this Your Honor. It's from Immanuel Kant: 'He who is cruel to animals becomes hard also in his dealings with men. We can judge the heart of Man by his treatment of animals.' What's in Chief's heart... is what saved me. Can we find that in our heart and do no less for him?"

She wiped her cheeks with the palms of her hands. She looked at them and saw that they were wet. She was sure it was sweat.

* * *

THE JUDGES DELIBERATIONS & DECISION

The door to his chambers opened and the judge came in; they rose as he sat.

"I've given this a great deal of thought. I've even gone and visited the dog... Chief," he nodded at Hannah and Constance, "over at the Animal Control facility. The laws, everything that has been cited previously by the District Attorney are clear." Henry Poindexter straightened and smiled already mentally writing his press release.

"But equally clear is the case at hand and situation where law, the laws as written conflict with what's right and have to be reinterpreted. It's not the province of this hearing, or within my powers, to change those laws. But it's clear that there are grounds to do so legislatively if the will is there. But what I can do is, as Ms. Wilkins put very well earlier in the proceedings, look at this from a different perspective. What we have here is someone—a person—who by all accounts has rendered a great service to the city and our state. And frankly, possibly, even other states and municipalities as it would appear this man now in jail has left a trail of dead and abused women across several states. So again, what we have is someone that's done such a good thing by not only saving Ms. Arshakunian, but also has prevented other brutal and heinous crimes from being committed. We could, and the media certainly should, call them a hero. And this person has been incarcerated without cause." He nodded at Connie.

"This is a complex matter as the dog, Chief, who has done this great service, is not a human being. But in this case, it is my opinion that he is in fact a person and certainly deserving of the rights and equal protection of a human being under our laws. I understand the furor my statement and opinion will cause. And I'll take that on my head and deal with it." He paused to pick up his notes, grouped, stacked and then set them aside. "Here's my decision. The person, known as Chief, shall be immediately released and returned to his friends and family."

The judge stood and smiled, holding his hands palm out to forestall any comments, complaints or celebrations. "As I said I thought about this a great deal. And a short while ago in my chambers, I called the Animal Control facility and asked them to bring Chief here. So that he reunites with those who love him, the one he saved and I think that saved him. Please bring him in."

Through a set of double-doors, a uniformed police officer pushed a pallet jack in front of him. On it sat a 5 x 5 metal cage on a wooden pallet. Inside, when Chief saw Hannah, he stood with his tail going like a windshield wiper set on high. The bailiff released the latch on the cage and swung the door open.

Hannah had risen and walked to the open area in front of the judge. "Here boy!" Shrugging off Connie's offer of help, she carefully lowered herself. She patted the floor next to her. "Here Chief... come here, buddy!"

In three bouncing steps, Chief leaped into her arms.

* * *

DENVER DISTRICT COURTHOUSE STEPS

They had come out into bright sunlight on the steps of the main entrance facing Bannock Street.

Hannah stopped with Chief at her side. There were at least two dozen dogs milling around on the steps. Most were leading their humans by their leash. "What the..." She exclaimed. "Who are these people?"

The people with the dogs saw them on the steps and the clapping started, then cheering and then barking. A lot of barking. She looked down at Chief who was bouncing on his feet. He looked up at her with his usual, tongue-hanging-out of the left side of his mouth, grin. Her dad, mother, Connie and Jon joined them on the steps with huge smiles on their faces. She looked over at Jon as a stout, pleasant looking, woman with long gray-streaked dark hair approached them. She had a young German shepherd on a leash. She handed that to Jon and he knelt and hugged the dog's neck.

"This is Wallace." He looked up at Hannah and then stood. "Troopers great, great-grandson." He put his arm around the woman. "And this is my wife Alicia." He kissed her smiling cheek. "She and Trooper saved my life."

"Did you..." Hannah swept her arms to take in all the men, women and dogs around them. "Do this?"

"Some of them are friends of mine. They convoyed here in motorhomes and campers..." He looked up and behind her. "I had help with finding some locals, too." She turned to follow his eyes.

"I can't tell you enough how pleased I am, Ms. Arshakunian." Adam Stockard stood on the same step as Hannah and was still two heads taller than she was.

He leaned down and the brim of his hat cast a shadow over her face. "Would you folks like an escort through the crowd?" He looked up to see three news vans pull up. "And past those guys?"

She followed his hand gesture at the media and saw the film crews unloading. One of the reporters leaned with difficulty in her tight red dress against one of the vans. She was using a rolled up piece of paper to scrape something from her four-inch heels. The disgusted look on her face confirmed that one of the dogs had left a present. Hannah turned from her and looked up into the sun and then at Adam and smiled. "Nope, I'd love to talk to them and introduce Chief."

20

JUNE 12, 2007
HANNAH'S PARENT'S HOME
STERLING, COLORADO

"ANYONE KNOW WHY A STATE POLICE PATROL CAR IS PULLING IN THE DRIVEWAY?" Hannah's mom dropped the curtain back into place and turned with a worried look on her face.

"No." Hannah and Connie answered her. Connie peeked out the window, too. Then looked at Hannah with a smile on her face.

"I think someone has a visitor." She commented in a singsong voice.

Hannah looked over her shoulder. "Don't be a smartass Connie." She gave her a stern look but inside she was smiling.

"I saw how he looked at you in the hearing and then afterwards. He's a big good-looking man." Connie snapped her gum.

Hannah's father was at the door holding it open. "Good to see you Adam; kind of surprised though."

Behind her, Hannah heard Connie snort, "I'm not."

"Shush..." But she didn't turn around to look at her.

"I thought I'd check in on you folks and see how you were doing."

He seemed uncomfortable standing there, awkwardly turning his trooper hat in his hands. Behind her, Connie snorted again as she greeted him. "It's nice to see you. I didn't think I would before..." she paused and looked at Chief who was sniffing the state trooper's legs, "we left for home."

The hat made three or four more rotations. "It's good to see you, too, Hannah."

One of the things she liked about him was that he always made eye contact when he talked to her. That was something she did, expected and respected in others. He seemed so genuine. "I'm glad you came by. Won't you sit and have a drink?"

"I can't do that since I'm on duty but if you're around this evening I'll take you up on that. And I have to admit wanting an opportunity to do that is why I'm here."

She heard Connie snapping her Wrigley's from across the room. Hannah thought she viewed the whole thing as entertainment; like watching one of those reality shows with her two dogs. Her mother was sitting next to her and both had wide grins. Her father was in his chair and smiling, too. She sighed and thought, all I need is Carol here to round out the rogue's gallery of people hyper-interested in my life.

"I want to thank you again for your help."

"Oh, that was all in the line of duty. I get deposed and have to make statements at trials and hearings all the time. It's part of the service ma'am." He made a gesture of putting his hat back on and tipping it at her.

"Well, thanks for that too, but I really meant about what you did to help round up the veterans, with their dogs, at the courthouse. I've never thought, even though I've done a lot of reading over the last few months, how much dogs have helped wounded veterans heal. And there's so many of both. So many dogs misunderstood, abandoned or mistreated and that lack a good home. There are many veterans like that, too and they feel hurt and alone. I know I did."

This time he did settle his hat on his head. "I know... But I hope your hurts and the pain are going away and that you know you're not alone." He gestured at everyone sitting and watching—their spectators—and at Chief, now asleep at her mother's feet while she stroked his head.

She had felt it building for a while and maybe now it had reached the brim. She had come home from war an empty shell of pain and regret. Slowly, bit by bit, the people that loved her filled it, replacing all the bad with good and all it took was one piece to nearly get her there... to where she felt she was a whole person again.

She looked at Chief snoozing so peacefully. "Maybe there's one final thing to do. One thing I need to try to find that's been missing." He looked at Hannah, unsure of what she meant. She smiled up at him. "What time are you going to pick me up for that drink?"

His grin was as big as his hat. "How about 7:30 tonight?"

She smiled and nodded. "Sounds good..."

And this time he did tip his hat.

EPILOGUE

NOVEMBER, 2014

THE STOCKARD'S HOME
SANTA CRUZ, CALIFORNIA

"WHEN WILL DADDY BE BACK, MOM?"

"Soon dear... the game's over now." Hannah marked the page in her book with a finger and reached down to tousle her daughter's sandy brown hair, so unlike her own. At least she wasn't hiding it under that old Colorado State Trooper's hat her father had given her. She was such a little tomboy. Right now, she was on the floor next to the new pit bull pup she'd insisted on naming Scooby. Next to her and the pup, by her feet on the other side, Chief was sleeping.

They had just finished watching the 49ers game. Though this year was tougher than the last couple of seasons Colin Kaepernick was still exciting to watch. She leaned forward and reached down to stroke Chief's head. He'd snoozed through most of the game.

"What are you reading mom?"

Finger in the book again to hold her spot, Hannah showed her the cover. "Marley & Me: Life and Love with the World's Worst Dog."

"What's it about?"

"A dog. And the woman and man who loved him."

Chief stirred as Hannah stretched to brush the top of his head with her fingers. He was over 10 years old now and slept a lot. The puppy came bouncing over and nuzzled him.

Her daughter rocked against her knee and looked up. "Read it to me! Tell me a story... Please!" Her grin—she had recently lost a front tooth—always melted Hannah's heart.

She glanced from her to the puppy that was now nose to nose with Chief. A series of low yips and yaps coming from him made Chief open his eyes. "Tell me a story grandpa..." Scooby nuzzled him again.

Chief raised his head to look at Hannah. She saw it and they looked at each other a long moment.

She nodded to him as she reached down and stroked his head some more.

"I'll tell you," she ruffled Amanda's hair, so much like her father's, "the story of a very brave dog that everyone rejected and no one loved; that saved a young woman's life... and how she saved his."

Chief looked at his grandson. "Listen to her young pup." With a deep sigh, he laid his head across Hannah's slippered foot and dreamed some more. He thought about acceptance, love, how happy he was and what he would like all humans to know.

> *"We pit bulls are labeled dangerous despite the statistics and facts that prove we are not. Lawmakers enacted laws to kill us, out of misplaced fear, without accurate information.*

> *That needs to be corrected; laws must be constructed to protect all sentient and feeling beings on our planet. I wish that someday, all animals are under the same, equal, protection afforded all human beings. That is what's right... that's what's fair."*

About the Author

After South Vietnam was delivered to the evil North in April 1975, after many failed attempts Duyen Nguyen finally escaped and came to the U.S. in November 1984. Mr. Nguyen was one of the almost 800,000 refugees known as, "boat people," half of which settled in the United States. He now practices law in San Jose, California. Mr. Nguyen is currently working on the re-publication of *Behind the Smoke Curtain*, a novel about the Vietnam war and on its sequel.

Coming Soon

Behind the Smoke Curtain
by Duyen Nguyen

Mai was a beautiful young Vietnamese girl and a student at Saigon University. Scott was a young American reporter trying to establish himself as a freelance writer and journalist. Where better to seek that chance than in a war-torn country full of stories every day.

They met and fell in love just before the Tet offensive of 1968, when it became shockingly clear to the United States that the conflict in Vietnam was far from over. Caught up in the lies, intrigue, betrayals and violence of the war, they suffered when Cold War opponents, behind their not so benign or altruistic curtain of diplomacy, pulled the strings of a nation in turmoil.

It is a sad and tragic truth that older men start the wars that the youth must fight and die. Told as only a person who lived in Vietnam during that time can tell; this is the story of Mai and Scott as they try to live and love while their world disintegrates around them.

Also From the Publisher:

THROUGH A LENS OF DARK & LIGHT

A NOVELLA

DENNIS LOWERY

Two letters from dead women...
A camera from a dead man...

That was all Robert Sterling, a once renowned photojournalist, had to guide him; to help him redeem and resurrect his life from two years lost in a drunken downward spiral. Was the young girl he could only see through the camera a ghost haunting him from a dead past or was she leading him towards a new future? Did she exist or was he going crazy just as his mother had forty years ago?

To find out, he had to go back to the small town he'd left nearly four decades years ago... a place he'd forgotten full of memories he'd buried. To where, when he was 18 years old, someone had tried to kill him for what he'd done. To where he found and lost his first love...

UNION & STATION

DENNIS LOWERY

She lived two lives...
And faced one killer...

Five days a week Elizabeth Holloway crossed the Great Hall through its morning setting of dark-to-light-to-dark again. Its vaulted skylight, above the enormous wooden benches, illumined some people and cast others in shadow. She wondered about those she saw in the same seat every day. Did those who sat in darkness have things to hide—as she did? She led two lives; one in the light, one in the dark. They started and ended at Union Station.

It was 1943... Dark times with a world at war... it was the kind of murder police didn't put more than a token effort into investigating. When a friend is killed and Beth finds she's next on the killer's list she has to take things in her own hands. Despite the risk of her hidden life being revealed... she has to avenge her friend and defend herself.

CPSIA information can be obtained
at www.ICGtesting.com
Printed in the USA
FSOW02n1936140415
6355FS